CREATRIX
RISING

UNLOCKING THE POWER
OF MIDLIFE WOMEN

STEPHANIE RAFFELOCK

SHE WRITES PRESS

Published 2021
Printed in the United States of America
Print ISBN: 978-1-64742-163-2 (paperback)
Print ISBN: 978-1-64742-318-6 (hardcover)
E-ISBN: 978-1-64742-164-9
Library of Congress Control Number: 2021903496

For information, address:
She Writes Press
1569 Solano Ave #546
Berkeley, CA 94707

Cover and interior design by Tabitha Lahr

She Writes Press is a division of SparkPoint Studio, LLC.

For Eva, Julia, and Cleopha

CONTENTS

INTRODUCTION

This is an extraordinary and significant time in feminist history. Women are starting to see the creative potential in their midlife years and beyond. Moreover, women are embracing this creativity in part because age is no longer seen as a burden but as an asset. Experience and hard-won wisdom count for something. Moreover, the women I know are exploring a deeper beauty. More than painting a pretty picture, this deeper beauty accentuates the qualities of their hearts and souls.

I wrote *Creatrix Rising: Unlocking the Power of Midlife Women* because I believe in you, the midlife woman who is emerging into this new time in history. I believe that women's struggle to gain equality has been courageous and in many ways victorious. And I think it's time we acknowledge our feminist history not just in the larger world, but in our own families and our own lives. Women have long been the keepers of stories, and the stories of women hold great power and great promise. When we reflect upon where we are in life, and where we've been, it can help us to map the journey forward.

I want to tell the story of what I'm seeing and feeling, and what I know to be a shared experience: midlife women actively claiming their greatness and standing in the light of leadership. We've walked a path from darkness into a bright new world, in spite of the obstacles we've faced. And now it's time to throw the stake into the ground and claim that we are reborn in all of our womanly glory.

I wrote this book in what will forever be known as the time of the Coronavirus pandemic. Few lives have been untouched by this momentous event. In the film *The Wizard of Oz*, Dorothy has a moment where she picks up her little dog and remarks, "Toto, I've a feeling we're not in Kansas anymore. . . ." If I'm no longer in Kansas, where the hell am I?

Change and creativity often grow from the mud of chaos. The word *social* in *social upheaval* implies that the course of direction is being altered by many groups. And that has been true during the time of Coronavirus. When the history is written about these times, the pandemic will be a marker for a great awakening of social issues. There is one event that feels especially important to me. It's positive, remarkable, and, in my eyes, quite extraordinary: the emergence of a new kind of woman, a new set of archetypal qualities assigned to women. It didn't start during the pandemic, but it did bloom. What's different about this particular evolution is that *we* are defining what those emerging qualities are, and we are owning them.

A new kind of woman isn't new in the sense that we've all been working toward a time when we would not be shy about our confidence or our power. We've all been working toward greater equality, while claiming the power within ourselves. But now we've hit a tipping point, a point of no return. We can never go back to qualities of coyness, submission, or silence as once assigned to us by the patriarchy. In fact, I think we are seeing a leveling of the playing field when it comes to the importance and impact of the matriarch and patriarchy, a kind of peaceful fairness that is settling over our culture in profound ways. It's not that we don't still have work to do, but women have definitely arrived!

As we become comfortable with the landscape of this particular Oz, we can see that women have grown into their courageous, confident, and strong selves. We understand that we have a crucial and sacred purpose in remaking our world. This is evidenced by seeing the women who run for political office and dare to lead. And it's evidenced by women in the Black Lives Matter movement, who paint with a wide brushstroke of healing, leadership, and instruction, the very things that will bring about social justice for all.

Our social environment has changed drastically, and women have risen to that occasion. Women are perhaps the best equipped to deal with the new world around us. They have been adapting to adversity and obstacles as a means to overcome them, and not be disheartened by them, for thousands of years.

Even though I came of age on the edges of modern feminism, much of my life has been defined by men and the ideas of men. One of the most extreme examples of this happened when I was in my midthirties. In June 1986, an issue of *Newsweek* utilized the power of a cover photo that depicted a graph of women's marriageability based on age. The article inside the magazine was titled "Too Late for Prince Charming?" It premised that single women over age thirty-five had a better chance of being killed by a terrorist than of finding a husband. Eventually the unpublished study upon which the article was based was completely debunked, and twenty years later *Newsweek* tried to do the honorable thing by retracting it. The idea crept into the culture nonetheless.

At the time the article was published, I felt the pangs of fear and anxiety. At thirty-four, I was unmarried, and according to the article, I was doomed. The *Newsweek* piece with its false theories was designed to do one thing, and that was put women in their place. Get married, make babies, and fulfill your only purpose in life—or die a lonely woman. That was the message. More than a few women over thirty-five married anyway, in spite of the warning.

By the 1980s, women had entered the workforce in droves, some opting to put a hold on starting families. The *Newsweek* article was an admonishment to career women, warning them that there was a price to be paid for competing with men in the workplace. The whole notion of marriageability hearkens back to a darker time in history when women were seen as property, a time when women were not thought capable of thinking for themselves, let alone living life on their own terms.

Women have been struggling to gain freedom for centuries. I've seen and lived the struggle in my own life, and I've also witnessed some of the benefits of that struggle. But once I turned fifty, I saw that in spite of my strong work ethic, strongly held value of continuing to educate myself, and well-earned confidence about my capabilities, I was once again on the outside looking in. The world in which I turned fifty wasn't all that friendly to older women. By 2002, I'd beat the *Newsweek* odds. I hadn't been shot by a terrorist, and I had married. As I lurched and staggered toward my own understanding of this milestone of a midlife age, I quickly realized there were two different standards and two different attitudes about age. The way that society viewed older men contained respect, along with continued opportunity. The manner in which older women were seen was fraught with defeminization and desexualization, thus rendering women insignificant and irrelevant in their later years.

In my sixties, I began exploring, through the process of writing, the potential greatness of being an older woman. I wanted to find a positive way to look at the accumulating years. As a blogger, I received comments and feedback from women my age who felt the way I did, that one's older years could be a place of reinvention, second chances, and taking on one's dreams. I met women who were physically active beyond what the stereotype says we can do. And I interacted with women who started new businesses in their fifties, becoming artists and activists.

In fact, none of the women I knew were comfortable with the worn-out definition of older women. The vitality and creativity birthed at midlife could not be silenced in this new kind of woman. What it meant to reach midlife had changed. Women were no longer willing to consider themselves too old to dream. I believe this to be true for most women in our culture: how we are seen by the world and how we see ourselves change when we turn fifty. Even at forty, we hear the bad jokes about being over the hill. Are women really used up, over the hill, useless after forty-five, fifty, fifty-five, or sixty? Is midlife *really* a crisis?

Recently, I looked up the term *midlife women* on the Internet. What came up were pages and pages of articles about midlife crisis. When, at midlife, we continue to seek living life on our own terms, are we having a midlife crisis? To dream and reinvent ourselves—is that *really* a crisis?

I have a friend who started an online business at fifty-five. Part of her business plan was to do a weekly podcast. She invested her time, energy, and money into her new endeavor, only to be asked by her husband, "Do you think you're having a midlife crisis?"

At midlife, women naturally experience a great surge of creativity but don't always recognize or acknowledge it. The only names we have for this period are *menopausal* or *midlife crisis*, neither of which carries a positive connotation. What about *midlife awakening*?

If you look around, what you see about midlife women is this: They run for political office in record numbers. They start new businesses. They write books. Most important, they don't buy into the male definition of who or what they should be as midlife women. Instead, they are finally living life on their own terms.

Living life on your own terms is midlife awakening.

~~~~~~~~~

The Book's Contents

Here is how *Creatrix Rising: Unlocking the Power of Midlife Women* unfolds to show the way for women coming into their power at midlife.

- *The prologue* sets the stage by describing traditional female archetypes, who established them, and how those models have defined our gender until now. A new archetype, the Creatrix, is introduced.

- *Part I, The Heroine's Journey*, contains stories about the women in my family: my great-grandmother, my grandmother, my mother, and me. My story is connected to theirs, just as your story is connected to the women in your family who went before you.

- *Part II, Creatrix Rising*, consists of stories about some of the personal obstacles that have challenged me and helped push me forward. I talk about how I learned to hold the passage of menopause in a new way, and how I came to live my life artistically and creatively.

- *In Part III, Embodying the Creatrix*, you'll find stories of women who lead by example, women who have integrated certain qualities of the Creatrix archetype and demonstrate them in strength and as a form of inspiration.

These stories are important because none of us become the women we were intended to be without drawing upon the help, friendship, and love of other women.

- *In the final section, Part IV, Celebrating the Creatrix,* the stories are about who we are beyond the influence of Madison Avenue or Wall Street, and how we can celebrate the deep beauty of our souls.

- *An epilogue* provides timely commentary and is based on a personification of the Coronavirus. It tells the story of how she (the virus) has changed our lives by challenging us to tend to what needs healing and what needs light.

At the end of each chapter, I offer questions and activities intended to inspire you to find, embrace, and grow into your own unique version of the Creatrix archetype. Feel free to respond to some, all, or none of them, as feels appropriate. My hope is that as you engage in these promptings, you will discover and then possibly tell your own amazing story— everything that has brought you to where you are now, whether the beginning, the middle, or the end of your midlife and midlife creativity. Within the questions we ask ourselves lies the purpose for exploring the power of our maturing years.

You may find you read a question and it stays with you throughout the day. You can parse your thoughts and feelings about the inquiry while you walk or go about quiet activity. Or you may want to journal or make notes. Everyone has to find what works best for them. It doesn't matter what method you choose. Just keep in mind the reason behind the questions: to nourish self-awareness, self-knowledge, and self-acceptance.

And finally, this is not a how-to book or self-help book, even though you may have found it in that section of your bookstore. More accurately, this is a book of personal stories and musings about coming to meet and know the emerging feminine archetype of the Creatrix. These writings are meant to inspire you to tell your own story about how you are claiming your voice as a mature woman, and to recognize how truly powerful, remarkable, and noble that is. The journey does not end in older years. In older womanhood, we continue to evolve until the very end.

Think of this book as a guide to your emergence into the most creative phase of your life, even more so than when you were the Mother. Now you are the mother to the world. It is my hope that you will be inspired to reflect upon your own stories and your own history. And just as I hope my book is a gift to you, I hope that you will be a gift to yourself. I hope you will gather the stories of ancient women to your heart, the stories that you live within every day, and the personal history of not only your story, or my story, but *the* story: the story of the sacred unfolding of women into the light of equality and personal power.

The Stage Is Set for the Creatrix to Emerge

Sometime in my forties, I became aware of a feminine archetypal model: Maiden/Mother/Crone. This model was meant to represent the summation of a woman's life in a way that all women could relate to. The Maiden was all about innocence and youth sitting at the precipice of womanhood. The Mother was self-evident—the time in a woman's life when she either bears children or engages in a professional career or calling. And finally, the Crone.

The word *crone* entered the lexicon six hundred years ago, around 1390. It means *disagreeable old woman*. Though some groups have sought to reclaim the word and dress it up as meaning *sacred* or *wise*, the etymology doesn't come close to suggesting that, so the word comes with cultural baggage. Crones are portrayed as old and ugly. They are defeminized and desexualized. They are used up, no longer capable of creating the one thing they've been allowed to create—babies. They are done and rendered irrelevant!

Contemplating the overarching journey of a woman's life—my own and that of many friends—is what drew me to this particular archetypal progression of Maiden, Mother, Crone. But as I explored the three phases, I realized there was something dreadfully wrong with how they progressed. The gap between Mother and Crone seemed much too wide. Something was missing.

I also had to question: Do we really still see older women the way people saw them in 1390? Was Crone even relevant at all?

I'm not a psychologist, sociologist, or theologian, and I can't lay claim to years of study with regard to this particular topic. But I am a storyteller, and I'm especially interested in the stories of women. Through the art of storytelling, I've learned a lot about the world and about myself.

As a storyteller, I know the universe is constantly presenting to us what we need to know. For instance, I can hear the wisdom of nature whispering to me when I walk in the woods, and I can hear my intuition speak to me in the early hours of the day as I write. One morning, it occurred to me that I knew the story of that missing phase that came after the Mother, and it was not the Crone. I was living in this as-yet-unnamed phase—and so were my friends. I could see "her" story everywhere, that woman who could no longer be called Crone. The potential of who we can be at midlife is so far beyond the intended insult of the word *Crone*.

I've written about aging for several years. I'm curious about how we see ourselves as we age and how the world sees us. As my realization of a new phase grew, I began to see certain cultural narratives in need of correction. The urgency to write about and claim what I was experiencing as the missing archetype that follows the Mother and replaces the Crone was getting louder in my head, fiercely demanding my attention.

I want to share a little bit of history here, some definitions and parameters that will help clarify and round out
my thoughts. Archetypes are universal, archaic ("age-old")
images that represent common human traits, expressions,
emotions, and experiences. They represent human potentials
that reside in the collective human unconscious until they
become activated within an individual, usually when certain
stages of life are entered. This activation can happen to us
consciously or unconsciously.

The energies and images of archetypes connect us by
allowing us to see ourselves in others. In the Maiden phase, we
recognize other maidens. In the Mother phase, we understand
and relate to other mothers. When stories contain wicked
witches, orphans, or queens, we have a unified understanding
of who those characters are and what they mean because their
traits are ones we know by heart.

One man who explored the archetypal definition of our
human experience was Carl Jung, a psychotherapist and
psychiatrist who practiced in the early to mid-1900s. Jung is
considered one of the most important figures in the history
of psychology. His analytic approach to understanding the
human psyche included stories and archetypes that he believed
served as clues to understanding the human condition. He
introduced the idea that archetypes were models of people,
behaviors, or personalities. To that end, he was a student of
mythology, literature, anthropology, art, and history.

The model of Maiden/Mother/Crone was not Jung's,
however. It belonged to the Irish poet and novelist Robert
Graves. Graves sketched out the phases of a woman's life in
an attempt to capture his muse, so Maiden/Mother/Crone
came from a man's idea of a woman's life. In Graves's case,
the feminine energy of the Maiden/Mother/Crone was what
served his poetic endeavor. He wrote about this in his 1948
book *The White Goddess*, in which he referred to the three

phases as the "triple goddess," each phase coinciding with a phase of the moon: the new moon represented the Maiden, the full moon represented the Mother, and the waning moon represented the Crone. The theology of the triple goddess took root in what is known as neo-paganism. Neo-paganism essentially amounts to nature worship, finding the divine in the temple of the natural world.

Graves should have stopped with the story he'd written to explain what he thought of as his muse, but instead he tried to fit the triple goddess and the phases of what he thought of as a woman's life into an ancient historical context. His efforts contained such glaring inaccuracies and untruths that *The White Goddess* was widely criticized when it was published. Nonetheless, like many ideas, there was a spark of possibility in his premise that allowed the idea to seep into the culture. And that's where our current understanding of Maiden/Mother/Crone comes from.

The idea that a woman's life is represented by phases, just as the moon waxes and wanes, inspires me. I have always related strongly to the notion that I am part of the natural world, and I hold a belief that the answers to all of my questions can be found in nature. Like Graves, I see the archetypes and their progression as a kind of muse, but with a major exception: We must acknowledge that Maiden/Mother/Crone is being redefined and rewritten all around us, this time by women. And we should celebrate that the phase Graves called Crone is being replaced by a new archetype for older women who are increasingly making their voices heard.

I've set out to reshape the tale of the Crone by including the archetype that's been missing to redefine how we think of older women. It's clear to me that the way we envision older women needs to be altered to reflect the evolution of our continuing liberation and growing self-awareness, equality, and confidence.

My generation came of age on the beginning edges of the modern feminist movement. I've never doubted that women had as much potential for a successful and satisfying life as men. At the same time, I sometimes blindly accepted the cultural assessment of who I was and who I thought I was supposed to be. Given this, some of the narrative that needs correcting has been my own.

Young women today forget, or maybe don't know, that in the fairly recent past, women could not get financial credit or loans without the signature of a husband, they were not admitted to prestigious universities like Yale until the late 1960s, and they struggled to get a foothold in professions that were predominately male.

Bless the rebellious women who pushed against these cultural norms—that sole female law student in a class of men; the female physician who bucked the system and somehow made it to the other side of medical school to rise above the stereotype of how women were seen in my generation. Those pioneers helped us all rise up individually and collectively to our greater potential. They carved out a path for the rest of us.

The evolution of strong women has educated us to the fact that we are always developing and can become more. Therefore, it seems that archetypes must evolve, too. Our lives are so much more than the summation of Robert Graves's muse, so much more than simply being here to serve a man's creativity.

When I look at women in our culture, I see the emerging archetype clearly. She is Carole King, Meryl Streep, Elizabeth Gilbert, and Reese Witherspoon. She is my next-door neighbor, a flourishing, vibrant woman. Are these women old? The answer has to be both a yes and a no, but then doesn't the word *old* deserve redefining, too?

Women in their fifties, sixties, seventies, and eighties are climbing mountains, making art, teaching, writing, and living lives that are full and engaged. They are creators of art—not "art" as a thing one does, but "art" in the sense of how one lives life. And there seems to be a theme for all these women: they give themselves to rich endeavors.

Life experience has taught me that when I'm trying to uplevel my game, it helps to name what I hope to achieve and then claim that achievement. *Name it and claim it.* That's the exercise. This unnamed archetype that I now see emerging in women all around me—what do I call it? I ran a list of names that might work: *Alchemist* because she creates something out of nothing. *Sage* because she's wiser now. *Transformer* because age is the great transformative event in life. But none of these names seemed to fit. The first two were distinctly masculine, and the third reminded me of a trailer for a kids' movie that showed cars turning into robots.

A friend mentioned the word *creatrix*. At first, I thought she was making it up, but as it turns out, *creatrix* is a real word, and unlike *alchemist* and *sage*, it is a word applied solely to women.

I propose that a new archetype, the Creatrix, is emerging with all of the qualities that support the reinvention, reimagination, and reawakening of strong, powerful women everywhere. *Creatrix* is a distinctly feminine word that simply means a woman who makes things. Women are making a new world with their power. It's not a power of conquering or the hierarchy of lauding over someone. Rather, it's the power of embracing a new identity starting at midlife by embodying the great creative surge that is a force for innovation and good in the world.

I see the Creatrix as a woman of forty-five, fifty, and beyond. She is who I feel in my heart. She is neither used up nor insignificant but is instead her own unique force of nature.

There is great clarity in knowing that the years you have left to live are less than those you've already lived. Such awareness nudges you out of complacency and imparts just enough urgency to help you get on with defining and living your ideal life. It's a power that generates second chances, encore careers, and especially a giving of one's self to the rapture of life's experience. The Creatrix archetype embodies this awareness, challenging us to find those gifts of age and hard-won wisdom that we can't imagine until our hands begin to wizen.

Here is how the progression needs to go: Maiden/ Mother/Creatrix. The Maiden becomes the Mother, and the Mother transforms into the Creatrix. The transformation into Creatrix is a vital and noble passage that establishes a new phase, one we are in until the very end. Unlike the Crone, the Creatrix is no haggard old woman of the forest. She has the radiant beauty we all seek, that of wisdom, compassion, courage, and strength. She is the witness that holds the lamp to illuminate the path the younger women behind her will traverse. The Creatrix is the pinnacle of a woman's life. As Carl Jung wrote in his 1933 book, *Modern Man in Search of a Soul*, "A human being would certainly not grow to be seventy or eighty years old if this longevity had no meaning for the species to which [s]he belongs. The afternoon of human life must also have a significance of its own and cannot be merely a pitiful appendage to life's morning." It is toward this wholeness that the Creatrix moves with a fierce grace and a bolder power for living fully in these later years.

The Creatrix says: Do not recede from life too soon, or retreat to some sparsely furnished waiting room that doesn't nourish and inspire your heart to "make things" during this phase.

If you look around you, you can see the Creatrix everywhere. Name her and claim her!

Part One:

The Heroine's Journey

I stood alone in the center of the room, the windows slightly open, letting in a cool breeze. Light streamed through the billowing curtains, making shadow play on the walls. I closed my eyes and saw the colors of bright orange and red behind my lids. Working with my imagination, my heart, and my intuition, I sensed my mother standing behind me. Then Grandmother Julia, standing behind her. Behind my grandmother was her mother, Great-Grandmother Eva. And so the line continued to stretch back behind me. Very soon, the faces blurred and the names were unknown, but the women were there nonetheless.

Each woman in my matriarchal lineage has contributed to my life, making me the person I know myself to be today. DNA and stardust: that's what informs the person I am constantly becoming. I'm still developing an appreciation and a love for those women, some of whom I've never met, but whose stories, real or imagined, are etched on my heart nonetheless.

I come from a family that's fragmented—a dream broken apart by fears and reasons I may never understand. Still, it's a family, though a little worse for wear. My family is rich with veins of love that have sometimes been hidden from me, the way veins of gold are hidden in a mine. It's an apt metaphor, because the process of self-discovery and awakening is very much a mining process. I've been willing to go deep, to dig around in the feeling and seeing places of my heart to know family that, in spite of all its brokenness, has given me the gift of learning. I've learned to be curious, to find gratitude in small things, and ultimately to forgive. I know that forgiveness stretches back in time along that line of mother and grandmothers, and then forward to one's own self. It's as if the circle has been mended and each woman made whole.

"What's past is prologue," Shakespeare wrote in *The Tempest*. I keep that in mind when I think of the women in my family. The stage was predetermined for them and kept them from exercising, or even being encouraged to exercise, their God-given potential. But in spite of cultural dictates, some of their greatness could not be squelched. My grandmother Julia only went through the third grade. Her family thought it was more important for her to work on the ranch than go to school. Besides, she was a girl, and what would a girl do with an education when what she needed to know was how to take care of a family?

My mother finished the ninth grade, and her parents, in turn, thought the family would be better served if she worked. As a young woman, my mother cleaned other people's homes, turning over her pay to appreciative parents who felt this was the best scenario for all concerned.

I became the first woman in my family to go to college and graduate. I've had so many choices and privileges not afforded to the women who came before me, but what I've learned is that each of those women, in their life experiences, helped pave the way for me. I like to believe they all had a desire for education and the liberation it can bring about. They were strong and resilient, but they were expected to be subservient to husbands. Theirs was not a world in which women talked of choices. That would be left to my generation.

I've done this exercise dozens of times. I face the windows, close my eyes, and feel the long line of ancestral women who stand behind me. I whisper a prayer of thanks for everything they continue to give me.

CHAPTER ONE

FEAR AND LOVE

My grandmother Julia's house was the last house on a
long ribbon of highway that led to a place where land
and horizon stretched tight across the Colorado sky. Giants
disguised as lilac bushes stood watch over her front yard.
They bloomed each spring, and their flowers were so heavy
and so sweet that when they bent down to meet me, they
blessed me while tickling my nose with a remembrance of joy.

Here, in a small house painted white, I spent hours with
my grandparents. The experience was one of love but also
fear. I'd recently lost my siblings and my dad in my parents' divorce. My brother and sister stayed with my dad in
New Mexico, and my mom brought herself and me to a
new home in Colorado, near my grandparents. Of course,
I couldn't have articulated it then; I was only six years old.
But being dropped off at my grandmother's house for a few
days evoked a terrible fear that I would lose my mom, too.
What if she never came back?

The nights were the worst of it. I'd lie awake watching
lights bounce off the wall from an occasional passing truck,

wondering if Mom was coming back to get me, as she had promised. When I couldn't stand not knowing for another minute, I'd tiptoe through the dark house to the telephone. The sound of the rotary dial was anything but quiet, but I'd pull the phone into the bedroom where I was supposed to be sleeping and close the door, hoping that my grandparents wouldn't hear me. I'd dial the number my mom had given me, but on the other end of the line, the phone just rang and rang without anyone answering my middle-of-the-night calls.

Did Julia know I was afraid? I don't recall that she ever demonstrated what I would call gestures of comfort. She wasn't a snuggler or a hugger, and she didn't say much. But in the morning light, Julia set in motion days that were filled with purpose and wonder, and following her through those days brought me solace.

The first time I stayed with her, it was summer. Each morning, after sharing coffee and biscuits at the kitchen table, our daily ritual, she would send me to the chicken coop with a basket to gather eggs. I loved getting the eggs. They were mostly blue and brown; only some of them were white like the kind you find in a grocery store. I liked talking to the chickens, believing they understood what I was saying. "Move over, brown chicken, I need to get the eggs in the back. That's a good girl." And I thanked them, telling them what beautiful eggs they'd made.

"I'll see you tomorrow," I said one morning as I backed out of the chicken coop and into the fenced area that was part of their domain. There was my grandmother, smiling at me. The chickens ran to her as she began to toss their feed onto the ground. While they pecked and scratched at their breakfast, Julia put a hand on my shoulder and led me through the gate. Eyeing my basket of eggs, she said, "Looks like those chickens were busy."

From chickens we'd move on to gardening. Kneeling by her side on the warm summer ground, wearing the apron she'd tied around my waist, we'd pick peas and beans, loading those green jewels into our upturned aprons before transferring them to large baskets. Throughout her garden were small statues of saints and angels, the size of something you'd put on a table or a dresser. Some were ceramic and others were sturdier, made of wood. The elements had not been gentle or kind to the statues, and as a result they were stained with spots caused by spring rains. The wooden ones had cracks here and there from the freeze and thaw of the winter months. Still, I believed the statues had a kind of power and magic in them, and I imagined that prayers in this garden of divinity went directly to heaven, where they were answered.

While we picked vegetables or pulled weeds, I was always careful not to disturb these small garden residents' homes. They stood on little mounds of rich soil or were tucked away under the blueberry bushes. Sometimes out of the corner of my eye, I could see my grandmother stop picking things and pull a rosary from her apron pocket. Closing her eyes, her face tilted toward the sun, she would rub the beads between her long, nimble fingers for a few minutes, her lips moving without sound. During those times, I was fascinated by her hands. I saw how they were thin and boney, how the skin was translucent. Veins and tendons looked like tree roots just below the surface of the skin.

Julia was the first older woman I ever knew or spent time with. Her hair was long and white. She often brushed it to one side of her face, wearing it in a long braid. Other times, she wrapped it into a bun at the nape of her neck. She always did her work in the garden, chicken coop, or barn in a flowered dress, even though a lot of what she did could have been done more easily in a pair of jeans. In the evenings, after dinner, we'd sit in the living room and watch television shows—*Perry Mason* was her favorite.

After a few days like these, my mom would come back and take me home.

I never knew when I was going to be sent off again to my grandparents. It must have been planned, because suddenly there we were again, a suitcase in tow and my mom encouraging me to go play outside under the giant lilacs while she and Julia whispered things I wasn't supposed to hear. Then she'd leave, and I would again be left with the unresolvable conflict of being afraid of my grandmother while loving her deeply.

One early winter morning after a big snowfall, I sat wrapped in a quilt in front of the coal-burning stove that heated my grandparents' house, watching intently while she stirred the embers and fed the flames. As the heat began to radiate into the room, she handed me a mug of hot coffee and milk. The two of us sat in silence, drinking our coffee while we grew warm and toasty from the fire. That day, she let me build a fort in front of the stove with two chairs and a blanket that created a roof and walls. I crawled in there with as many pillows as I could find and read old comic books that Julia had saved from when my cousins were little.

Inside my fort, I could smell soup simmering on the stove. I could hear my grandpa, Paul, as he stumbled out of his bedroom in the early afternoon, and my grandmother's voice scolding him, asking him was it worth it and had he slept it off? The demons of alcohol kept a tight rein on the sad man who, like me, looked for comfort from the inevitable losses that accompany life. My grandparents would be gone for decades before I understood that none of us escape the presence of grief in our lives and we handle it each in our own way, whether it's alcohol or a garden of saints.

When I was fourteen years old and no longer spending days at a time at my grandparents' house, my grandfather died. By then I'd grown very fond of the old man who often drank too much. I'd taken delight in sitting with him on an old chair behind the barn while he sipped on a bottle of Jack Daniel's and regaled me with stories about horses and trains that had taken him places.

Today it was a hearse that was taking him to a place where he would sleep forever. I rode in the funeral limousine, my mother on one side of my grandmother and me on the other. My aunt Ann sat across from us with one of my cousins. Mom and my aunt kept asking Julia what she would do with the farm, suggesting it might be a good time to sell the property and move into a more modern house closer to town. My grandmother didn't comment or answer. Instead she rested her head on my shoulder and took my hand. I leaned into her, the two of us finally able to comfort each other in a way that involved the gentle touching of hands, as kindred spirits who truly loved one another.

What I didn't know then was that there would be only three more years after the funeral when Julia would be part of my life. Mom and I left Colorado and moved to Arizona after Julia sold the farm and gave all of her children generous cash gifts with which to buy houses. All during the farm sale negotiation, Julia's daughters complained that she was too old to get a good deal for herself, insisting that one of them should intervene. But in the end, Julia got a lot more money for that farm than anyone would ever have imagined. She knew the value of what she had built.

I only stayed in Arizona for a year. The mother I'd once been so afraid to lose now drove me crazy on a regular basis, and I couldn't wait to get away from her. I never saw Julia again. She died shortly after I left home, and I didn't have the resources or stability to make it to her funeral.

Then, as I approached midlife, Julia took up residence in my psyche. I hadn't realized how much she cared for me and helped me when I was that little girl whose family had just broken into a thousand little pieces. I can't trace the spirit of Julia reentering my life back to a single event. Maybe it was as simple as becoming mature enough to see how remarkable she had been—an older woman without apologies, fierce in her independence and her love for creation and all growing things.

Julia is still with me, guiding me, reminding me of stories from our shared past, letting me know that strong women don't get weak with age; they just get strong in other ways. That's why I begin my story with her. I am the age now that she was when I first established a relationship with her. The way she lived her life made it very clear to me that growing older is a noble passage—not because we're finally old enough to get things right, but because we finally know there's no destination point. In spite of age, or maybe because of it, our last chapter contains the truth that we can continue to grow and change until the day we die.

I learned many things by watching my grandmother Julia go about her days and live her life on her own terms. No words of explanation were needed. The beauty of being older, I learned, is that we continue to unfold and give ourselves more fully to love right up to the edges of eternity.

For Reflection, Activity, and Journaling

Here are some questions and activities intended to inspire you to find, embrace, and grow into your own unique version of the Creatrix archetype.

1. After reading the story about my grandmother, do you recall specific stories about your own mother or grandmother that influenced and informed your life? What are some of the ways you were inspired by them? What was the life lesson that was imparted to you?

2. Think about a woman who embodies the Creatrix archetype that you know now or have known recently. How does her life inspire you to your own greater creativity at midlife?

3. *Creatrix* literally means "a woman who makes things." How do you make things in your life? Do you, as the late John Lewis said, "make good trouble"? Is social activism a path for you? Art? Gardening? Creating spaces of comfort for yourself and others? What do you "make" in the world—or want to make?

CHAPTER TWO

FINDING EVA

When she reached out to me that day, I followed her whisper along the ridge of brittle grasses bent back by the Colorado wind. Followed something that felt like the sound of ancient women dancing, rattling silver and bones at the mouth of a cave. I could feel her urging me to open myself to the invitation, to set aside doubt and disbelief. A strange sensation of satisfaction washed over me: *I've been found.*

Isn't this what family does when someone dies? They invite you in and give you cold cuts and consolation. My great-grandmother Eva didn't have cold cuts, but she did offer me consolation.

I'd been driving toward the highway, a silent struggle churning inside of me. I was wondering where I fit in or if I belonged to anything, anyone. That's when Eva called to me. A sign above the arched iron gates read ELBERT CEMETERY. The pull to her was so strong that I took the sharp left off Elbert Road without even thinking about it.

My brother, his daughter, and another of my mother's granddaughters were with me. We had just scattered the ashes of my mother on a hillside near the small town where she grew up. I'd called someone on the Elbert City Council, and they'd put me in touch with a sympathetic rancher who told me I could scatter the ashes on his land. The hillside was outside the bounds of that, but it didn't seem to be anyone's land, just the open space that one finds in an area of ranches and foothills. We'd all agreed that it looked like the right place—a hill of pine trees and rock outcroppings with a view of distant plains. We found the spot after driving around for a half hour looking for where we should spread the ashes that rode in a fabric box in the trunk of my car. I'd put together a wicker basket—a funeral basket that contained her ashes and a few other items.

For me, the area of pine trees we'd decided upon was reminiscent of an old family photograph. In the picture, my great-grandmother Eva is holding an infant on her lap. Her stern-looking husband, Jon, is standing behind her, and posed around them are seven of their nine children, including my grandmother, Julia. There are no smiles, just their eyes looking directly into the lens. The picture would have been taken sometime in the late 1800s when my great-grandparents were settling in this new country from Polish Russia.

None of us had ever been to the little town of Elbert, Colorado, before. It's where my mother and her siblings were born, the place she recalled when she told me stories about riding her horse Duke away from the hills and out onto the plains. Of all her life stories, the ones that took place in Elbert were her happiest, so that's where I thought she should be laid to rest. I'd brought her home, back to her family.

My siblings hadn't wanted a funeral for our mother, and I was left sad and embarrassed that one more time, the life events that were supposed to bring families together were tugging at whatever frayed tethers were left of ours, threatening to tear us further apart. Between my siblings and I, an old, simmering anger was always on the back burner of our collective family psyche. It held the story of how my mother left my father and took me, leaving my brother and sister behind while she and I moved to another state. With the exception of my earliest years, I never knew the consistency or continuity of a family unit. Neither did they.

As a kid, I would go for years at a time without seeing or hearing from my siblings or my father. I belonged to my mother. She was the person who was there day to day. She was all I had, and that I grieved her loss was difficult to explain to my brother and sister. She'd once left them behind, and that was a wound that had never healed. I had my own grievances with her but needed to do something to mark her passing. After I talked with my brother, he said he'd come, but only for me, not for her. My sister stayed in Arizona, dealing with things in her own way.

I wrote out for myself what I thought a funeral should look like, because that's what I do: I write things out, hoping to make some sense of what's happening, to slow my mind down enough to get to the emotion of the matter. I wrote a poem and printed it on cardboard stock with a picture of her alongside the text—a memory card, similar to one I'd seen at another funeral, to be distributed to each person present. But it all felt awkward, like I was trying to imitate what other people do.

"What did you do this weekend?"

"I made up a funeral for my mother."

"Isn't that what the funeral place is supposed to do?"

"We didn't have a funeral place, just the ashes. My sister FedExed them to me."

"Is it what your mother wanted?"

"I don't know what she wanted, but I believed she deserved to be honored."

"It's good then?"

"I think so. . . ." And that's how the conversation went in my head.

Once we'd found the place and walked up the hill with the funeral basket, I carefully unwrapped the box that held her ashes. I handed my niece a copy of "The Lord Is My Shepherd" that I'd printed off the Internet. She read it aloud while I scattered the ashes.

Surprisingly, the wind lifted the ashes, and they swirled upward like sparkling dust. Some of them blew back onto my shoes, sticking to the suede, a grayish kind of dust not as sparkly as what had floated into the sky.

I read the poem I'd written, and then handed my brother and nieces the memory cards. Then it was over, and none of us really knew what to do. We hugged each other. We lingered on the hillside for a while, each of us lost in our thoughts. I was relieved and grateful that I'd gotten to say what felt like a proper goodbye. Within the ritual I'd created was the sweet balm of forgiveness along with a kind of humility that recognizes no matter how well or poorly one lives their life, in the end, it's reduced to dust and memories. My brother had said he'd come to Elbert for me, not for her. Later he shared with me that he hadn't realized how much he'd needed to be part of the formal goodbye.

We had driven a couple of hours outside of Denver to find the town of Elbert and conduct our ceremony. A stream followed Elbert Road, flanked by trees that were turning orange and gold, as if this place had opened itself to greet us. This memorial had been punctuated by the colors and textures of an autumn day. As we lingered for a few more minutes on the hillside, I whispered a little prayer to myself: "May this connection, this tenderness never leave us." Without a word, we made our way back to the car to drive home.

That's when I heard Eva calling me.

Eva Lache-Baginiski, my great-grandmother, died in 1928. My mom told me her grandparents were buried in Elbert Cemetery, and I have to believe it was Eva who called to me and made me take that sharp left off Elbert Road to the arched iron gates marking the entrance to the cemetery. Otherwise, how would I have managed to park my car just a few yards from her grave? It was as if we all knew where we were going, walking up to the heavy granite slab that held the engraved names of our ancestors: my great-grandmother Eva and my great-grandfather Jon, along with markers for children who didn't make it very far into life and great-uncles whose names were new to me. To this family, she'd invited us in.

On that day, Eva started to live inside of me, just the way my grandma Julia did. I'm not the only woman who claims to have felt her ancestors walking with her, whispering to her. I'm not the only woman who feels connected to the spiritual DNA of her ancestors, the ancient women who sang ancient songs. The connective tissue of my family was a mystery fraught with abandonment, secrets, and betrayals. Somehow in death, all of that dissolves. Eva welcomed me. Her mother, Anna, stood behind her. My mother, Cleopha, and my grandmother Julia were there. They were a place and promise of my true belonging. I was of the same hardy stock of Polish women who had crossed oceans and continents, and were now coming alive in my heart and imagination.

It wasn't just me that Eva welcomed in that day. I believe she was there to welcome my mother, too, as well as my brother and nieces who stood beside me at her graveside. I couldn't tell if they were under the same spell that I was, and I didn't ask if they felt Eva's calling as I did. What I knew for sure though was that finding our ancestors' graves on the same day that we scattered our mother's ashes seemed to be a sacred event for all of us.

I only have the one photograph of Eva, the one with the seven children around her. Her children grew up, and eventually each of them moved away from Elbert. My grandmother

Julia had once told me that there was no work in the small town in which she had married and started a family.

Who did Eva become after her children were grown? I think that would have seemed like a luxurious question to her. The only evidence I have of who Eva was could be seen in the fierce independence of Julia. It could also be seen in my own mother, an even more independent woman than those who'd come before her. Eva was in me, too, the girl who came of age on the edges of feminism and was afforded the opportunities of education and choice in ways Eva herself had never known.

The contributions of Eva, Julia, and my mother, Cleopha, cannot be underestimated in how they each made the path a little bit easier for me. Breaking trail is slow and courageous work. And we, women of today, still have trail to clear.

I have tears for Eva. They are tears of joy that she came to me on a day that I most needed the comfort and wisdom of an older woman. It's a gift to know in some physical or psychic way the women who came before us. It makes us feel the importance of being a light and a blessing to other women. It brings forth the desire to welcome in the weary and be someone who uplifts. When I let go of this world, I'm hoping that just for a moment, I will brush up against the long line of women who came before me, and that I will be able to look into Eva's eyes and say how proud I am to be her great-granddaughter. Then the wind will lift me up, and I will be sparkling dust rising to the sky.

For Reflection, Activity, and Journaling

Here's an exercise you can do to bring you closer to the women in your life who went before you.

Write down three questions you have of your mother or another important woman "who went before," whether alive or not. Close your eyes and breathe in three deep breaths, and see if you feel, sense, or hear her answers.

When my mom died, I was struck by how piercing the absence was. What surprised me was that although she had died, the relationship didn't end. In fact, the relationship continued. She died in September, and in December a geranium that was in my kitchen window bloomed in a way that covered the windowsill in a carpet of deep pink flowers. I can't tell you how, can't tell you why, but I always believed that the blooming of the plant in the dead of winter was a final goodbye from my mom. It was then that I began talking with her and would sometimes hear her whisper back.

I do this conversation exercise with my mom when I'm trying to remember what she put in her stacked enchiladas, when I'm hiking through the woods, or when I'm around my friend's horses. I talk to her sometimes silently in my heart and sometimes aloud. We've become closer over the years, and the grievances that I had with her as a young woman have disappeared, never to be reclaimed by either of us.

Chapter Three

A Price to Be Paid

My mom would never call herself a feminist. She was all about the lace and lavender. Her life instructions ranged from "A lady never goes out of the house without a hat and gloves" to "Never cook fish when a man comes to dinner—it smells like sex, and it will give him ideas." God, the 1950s were scary.

Nonetheless, my mom, who went by Cleo, was a single, working mother at a time when there weren't too many of those. And although she never relinquished the coquettish habit of lowering her head and looking at you from underneath her long eyelashes, the hat and gloves came and went as her identity changed. I can't speak to the fish. . . .

A divorce made her a fallen woman in my grandmother's eyes, and that filled my mother's eyes with sadness. It wasn't like today when the dad would take the kids for the weekend. There were fewer than half a dozen visits with my father when I was growing up. Early on, he moved across the country, and it took hours by plane to reach him.

Raising me was strictly my mother's business, and the odds were stacked against her in an unfriendly way. *Fallen woman. Divorce.* Neither of those terms were said with anything but disdain. I learned early on that the divorce was her fault, and I never really understood what that meant. What about my father? Didn't he have some part in it, too?

In the 1950s and '60s, most of my friends had stay-at-home moms who made sure that cookies and milk were ready when they came home from school. I came home alone to an apartment every day. I was a latchkey kid before the term was ever coined, and it was because my mom was working. Our routine was different. I would call my mom at the office when I got home from school. Then I'd put the phone down while she waited on the line, and I'd look in all the closets and all the rooms before telling her that everything was fine. The ritual scared me. What if someone was there? Would she hear me scream, hang up, and call the police? I hated the ritual, and we eventually dropped it, but by then I was in junior high school.

Mom had been trained for virtually nothing except being a wife and mother, and while those are tough jobs, carving out a living for us at a time when there weren't many women in the workforce was her greatest challenge, as well as an uphill battle.

When we were first on our own, Cleo had never worked at anything other than being a housekeeper as a teenager. But she soon began checking the newspaper daily, circling ads and looking for something she thought she could do. One day she answered an ad in *The Denver Post* that read: "Skip tracer wanted for bail bondsman." She had no idea what that meant but called the number anyway. It was an early lesson for me that sometimes in life you just have to fake it till you make it.

A bail bondsman is the guy who posts bail for someone accused of a crime so they can stay out of jail after they get arrested. The bigger the crime, the bigger the bond. If the accused doesn't show up for a court date, the bondsman has to pay money to the court. Sometimes people would skip their trial and leave town. My mom learned to track them down and bring them back for trial.

Cleo had a knack for finding people, had a flair for asking for money. The bail bondsman loved her, and she was happy to have a job. Some of Denver's finest criminals marched in and out of the office where she worked. Cleo was in her late thirties by then, and what a looker. The bad guys had a soft spot in their hearts for the hat-and-gloves kind of woman she was. More than one of them told her that if she ever needed anything at all, they'd get it done, and that if anyone ever gave her any trouble, she should let them know, and they'd take care of it for her.

In my adult life, I became a Raymond Chandler fan. Chandler was a writer who crafted gritty mysteries and thrillers in the 1930s. I often imagined my mom as a character in one of his novels. She'd be the beautiful, hard-hitting dame, a secretary who made men weak in the knees. She'd be the smart one that solved the crime, and without her, catching the bad guys would have been impossible.

It wasn't until the early 1960s, when John F. Kennedy was still president, that Cleo made an upward move to handling collections at a large sporting goods store in Denver. It was a big move because the store had three locations, and she was in charge of collections for all of them. She bought a new hat to celebrate. I always thought that my mom looked like a model when she wore a hat. These weren't church hats or schoolteacher hats. These were hats with feathers that tickled her chin, hats with half veils that made her seem mysterious, and hats rimmed in fur that matched the collar on her coat.

In those days, there weren't any big chains, but instead a kind of local flavor that could only be found in your own town and not on every street corner in America. In that environment, my mom became the head of collections for a handful of sporting goods stores, and she wore that title with deserved pride.

She liked her job. Liked the people. Felt smart, and some of what was left over from her lavender-and-lace days gave way to trim black pencil skirts and crisp white blouses, accessorized by sharp high-heeled spectator shoes. The way she looked when she left for work in the mornings made me proud. And I wanted to be just like her when I grew up. Smart and in charge.

After a few years, the owners hired an assistant for her. At home, during our dinner conversations, she'd tell me how she'd delegate certain tasks to him, and how that helped her do a better job and ultimately helped the company.

When I was eleven years old, she came home from work one day, took off her shoes at the door, and fell onto the couch, crying. "I quit my job today," she said.

"Why?" Even at eleven, I knew that money was tight. Mom worked hard to "make ends meet," as she was fond of saying. "Why did you quit?" Fear was already turning my belly into a knot.

"I found out that they were paying my assistant more than they were paying me."

I didn't understand the way she'd answered my question. If my mom had been at the job the longest, and she was the head of everything, why was her assistant making more money than she was? "That's not fair," I said. "You should tell them." I could feel my voice start to shake, and I felt so lost that I couldn't help or comfort her. "Tell them. Maybe they made a mistake."

She sat up on the couch and wiped her eyes. "They didn't make a mistake," she said. Fishing out a handkerchief from her purse, she blew her nose. "I did tell them," she said. "When I found out, I went to my boss and asked him if it was a mistake. He shook his head at me and shrugged his shoulders, and just said, 'Well, Cleo, he has a family to take care of.' I just stood there looking at him, and finally I said, 'So do I.' I walked back to my office, hoping he'd follow me, but he didn't."

Then she started to cry again, but quietly. Tears just rolling down her face, wiped away with the sleeve of her crisp white blouse. "We'll be okay," she said.

My heart broke for her. It was so terribly, terribly wrong. What happened wasn't fair, and I understood why she'd quit. It was the first time I realized women were treated differently than men in the workplace. Long before there was a Lilly Ledbetter Act, before there was ever the battle cry of "equal pay for equal work," Cleo took the only dignified action afforded her. She stood on principle, and she quit. And even though I knew it wasn't right that quitting was all she could do to make a point, I was proud of the decision she'd made. I shared in the sorrow of the injustice that day, but part of me was also proud of her strength and resolve.

As she promised, we were okay. My mom's next job was with a large hospital as the head of their collections department. Even though the pay was better, I couldn't help but be a little afraid for her. After all, there was little recourse for the injustices of the workplace. She worked at the hospital until she left Denver.

Shortly after I moved away from home, my mother met and married her second husband. He didn't encourage or support her strong work ethic. He didn't see her as smart and capable. I didn't like him, though my mom seemed happy to retire. I think she was tired from the battle. I'm not sure she ever realized she was someone who helped pave the way for other women being in the workforce.

She settled into her new married life. When I visited, I discovered that she'd returned to the woman who was all about the lavender and lace. I missed the woman in the black pencil skirt and crisp white blouse, but there was no way to bring her back. She'd been my heroine, my favorite incarnation of a mom, a reliant and courageous woman who bucked the system and stood in the light of her truth—at least for a time.

It nourishes me to remember that the women who came before me did not have the same privileges and opportunities that I've had. They were busy carving out a better path in reality and in dreams for those who would follow them. Each of them, in their own way, made my path easier, made my ideas seem more significant.

It took me a while to understand that my fierce independence was something that I'd learned from my mom. She modeled principle and strength and a willingness to take risks and speak up for herself. I don't think those cookies-and-milk moms could have given me that. I don't know if I would have learned that speaking up for myself is not only an act of courage, but also an act of great self-love.

For Reflection, Activity, and Journaling

The workplace has long been a magnifying glass for showing us the price women have paid to become more independent. Courage in the face of inequality is the way the road was forged for us. Whether it was fighting for the vote, for equal educational opportunities, or within family structures, women have never given up the vision of creating life on their own terms.

1. Can you think of an older woman you've known whose courage and bravery made a deep impression on you? How was that woman paving a way to make your way smoother? What was she striving for? What was she fighting for?

2. What has your work or career choices taught you about yourself? How do you think you are paving the way for the women who will come after you?

3. Was there a time when you were frustrated with the inequality you experienced in work environments? Did you feel that you could do anything about it? Did you feel that you could rise above the inequality and make a difference?

4. How has your work informed a greater or lesser sense of independence in your life?

Chapter Four

Everyone Has a Place
Where the Journey Begins

I shut the door slowly and held my breath. I heard the latch click, and then I turned the dead bolt on the door of my new apartment. I had just waved goodbye to my mother as she pulled away in her powder-blue Mustang and headed back to Phoenix. Standing at the curb, I watched the car move down the street, getting smaller and smaller until it turned, and she was gone.

The way I liked to tell the story was that I ran away from home. The truth is, I didn't really run away. My mother drove me. She drove me from Phoenix, Arizona, to Los Angeles, California, where she paid one month's rent on an apartment, bought me a set of towels, filled the fridge, and returned to Phoenix. It was 1969 and I was seventeen years old, a high school dropout with no idea how to do life. Even though I'd assured my mother I could take care of myself, I didn't really know if I could.

I see seventeen-year-old girls now, and I think, *That's how old I was when she left me.* But I've always been confused as to whether my mother or I was to blame. How could a mother drive her underage daughter to a city like Los Angeles and just leave her there? How could I have asked her to drive me there and then leave me, to let me be on my own and begin a career as a singer-songwriter? There was no career, and I didn't know where or how to begin getting one.

Los Angeles had a shitty bus system, and I didn't have a car. Somehow I managed to make my way around. I thought about getting a job as a waitress but didn't know how. Maybe a salesclerk, but I didn't know how. It dawned on me fairly quickly that I was screwed. I had a little bit of cash—maybe a few hundred dollars, but that was it.

I can't remember now how I got an appointment with a record producer at RCA to sing him some of the songs I'd written. He was twenty-eight years old to my seventeen. I sat in his office, singing my compositions, as he listened and smiled at me the entire time. When I finally laid my guitar down, he said, "We should do a demo. I think I could use a couple of those songs."

Yes, please God, please, use a couple of my songs. I have rent due in two weeks and no job. I don't know what to do when the refrigerator gets empty. How will I buy groceries? I don't have a car. I'm lonely and afraid. Inside my head I screamed all of that. Outwardly I smiled back at him. "That would be great. When do you want to do the demo?" I asked.

Ray. He was tall. He had thick, dark hair that grazed his shoulders and muttonchops that made him look like the coolest guy in the world. He wore a strand of love beads around his neck—carved wooden beads, with shellacked shells scattered throughout. I wanted to touch them.

"Do you want to smoke?" he asked me.

"Cigarettes?" My answer made him laugh, and I laughed, too.

"Come on," he said, taking me by the hand.

"What about my guitar?"

"Leave it here. We'll come back."

We sat in his gold-colored Pontiac in the parking garage. He filled a pipe with grass, lit it, and handed it to me; I didn't tell him that I'd never smoked grass before. I took the pipe and pulled the smoke into my mouth before letting it out.

"No," he said, laughing again. "You have to breathe it into your lungs and then hold it there."

I tried again, breathed it into my lungs, and held my breath before I started coughing uncontrollably. He took the pipe from my hand.

Taking a long hit, he motioned me closer to his mouth, and when I got there, he gently breathed the smoke into me, and I breathed it back into him. When we stopped, he smiled again and touched my cheek. "Like that," he said, just before he kissed me. *Oh my God.* He was so handsome, and I needed a savior.

What will I do when the rent comes due in two weeks? When the fridge is empty? I'm low on cash. I don't have a job. I don't belong anywhere.

My guitar stayed in his office. I went home with him. I'd only ever been with high school boys, fumbling awkwardly in the back seat of a car. I didn't really know what it was to lie down next to someone and be wrapped up in their body. And I didn't know until that night that lovemaking could be so complex, so beautiful. So many things that could be done to me, that could take me away to where I was drowning in sensuous touch and emotion.

It must have been the weekend, or maybe a holiday, because it was three nights like this. Bed. Pot. Sex. Food. Bed. Pot. Sex. Food. So little said. So little that needed to be said. At two o'clock one morning, he woke me up. More sex, and then he led me into his music room, where I sat on the floor listening to him play the piano, thinking it was the most beautiful music I'd ever heard.

He called a cab for me the morning he went back to work. "Come by later," he said, putting a couple of hundred dollars into my hand. "Cab fare." He winked at me, touching my cheek.

This was how I lived for two weeks. Cabs to and from his house. Pot. Sex. Food. All in his bed. He brought me into the recording studio with him, let me sit behind him as he sat at the giant mixing board. Put me on the couch when he was conducting string and horn sections so that I could watch through the glass. And I sat so quietly, being so good. *I'm running out of food. The rent is almost due. I don't know how to get a job. I'm drowning in you. What am I supposed to do?*

The end of the month came. I was alone in my apartment. Ray was in the studio. I counted the money I had left. Enough to pay the rent, leave a note, and tell the landlord that I'd be gone. I put the cash in an envelope with my note. I packed my things in two suitcases and two boxes that I'd gotten from the corner liquor store. I called a cab. Just enough money left for the cab.

The cabdriver set my bags and boxes in Ray's driveway. I let myself in through the gate to the backyard and climbed in through the bathroom window. Retrieving everything from the driveway, I arranged things in his house, hung my clothes in the closet in the music room, vacuumed the floor, and washed the dishes in the kitchen. I changed the sheets on the bed and slid my freshly showered body under the covers.

I didn't hear the front door open at five in the morning. I didn't hear when he gasped and then laughed out loud. But I felt the bed move when he sat on the edge and began stroking my hair. "How'd you get in?" he asked.

"Through the bathroom window."

"Protected by a silver spoon?" he laughed, referring to the Beatles song.

I extended my arms to him. *My rent was due. I'm out of cash. There's no more food in my apartment. I don't know what to do.*

He pulled me close to him. "Stay with me," he said.

I started to cry. He held me tighter. "My phone was disconnected because I didn't pay the bill."

"Stay with me," he said again. "Stay forever."

✦　✦　✦

The first time we dropped acid, we stayed up all night. We made love. We laughed, hysterical laughter that wasn't about anything. Maniacal laughter. I couldn't catch my breath. I saw things on the walls. I saw colors around him. Things swirled and melded and morphed. I told myself the universe was opening to me and making me bloom.

As we started to come down from the peak of our high, my jaw hurt. I'd been grinding my teeth, because that's what acid does to you. You get so wired and ramped up that you grind your teeth. At 7:00 a.m., with a sore jaw and an aching back, I felt like I understood everything. Literally everything in the universe. Acid does that to you, too. We got dressed and drove into Hollywood. We stood in line at a theater that was showing the Beatles movie *Let It Be*. At least that's how I remember it, but maybe it was another Beatles movie. I can't tell you that I really remember the movie.

Ray whispered in my ear, "All of these people have been up all night. Can't you tell? They've all dropped acid."

Had they? I looked around me. When I see myself now, standing in line at that movie theater that morning at eight o'clock . . . when I see myself from this many years away, I see a waif of an unkempt girl who isn't eating much because so many of the drugs she is taking suppress appetite. She's too thin. Her eyes are too dark, and her pupils too big. She's physically exhausted, but she's so numb she doesn't know it. She lives in a perpetual state of confusion and chaos. I want to cry when I see her. How could I have been so cruel to her? To the gift of that life? How could my mother have left me? How could I have asked to be let go?

I want to take her into my arms, the waif from that time. I hated her for so long. I hated every choice she made, everything she stood for. How is it that courage crept into her life, and over time she found therapists and ministers and a college education that pulled her out of all that? How is it that she survived and found true love? She is so broken, and for too long I hated her, didn't give her any love at all. Ignored her existence. I became the mother, driving away in the powder-blue Mustang. I became the one who abandoned her.

Someone else might have given up, but my younger, lost self, stripped too soon of innocence, found her way out of that world. She dedicated herself to AA meetings, the only game in town, because in those days, there weren't any meetings for drug addicts.

It's said that time may not be linear. Could it be that everything in our life—past, present, and future—happens simultaneously? If time does happen all at once instead of events following one after the other, then I can imagine my sixty-eight-year-old self and my younger, reckless self meeting each other. There's an odd sense of comfort in imagining that she might know me, might see what she would become. And if we could experience each other that way, I would want her to witness me applauding and encouraging her courageous journey.

I look back, and it's in imagination only that I view her through a different lens, wishing that she could feel a sense of peace that life wouldn't always be so harsh. I saw the risks that the younger me took to write songs and sing them for people, an awkward attempt at expressing the pain and confusion of her life. I realized the determination and will that it took when she left Ray. Little by little, she conquered her addiction. The risks continued but the recklessness stopped.

No one should be faced with the kinds of choices I had to make at seventeen years old. It's the hardest part of my life to write about, to admit that I made stupid choice upon stupid choice upon stupid choice. Yet the day came when I knew I had to articulate what had happened inside of me when my mother drove me to Los Angeles and left me there. Nothing felt right. Nothing felt real. Nothing felt. I was trying to be a grown-up, trying to be cool, and none of it worked. Drugs were my comfort in life. *Don't worry*, they said. *You don't have to feel anything.*

Speed can keep you up for days. LSD, too. Pot is just the in-between. Chaos. Blur. Chaos. Blur. And one day, I turned twenty-one. Ray screamed at me. I screamed at him. We didn't hit, but we threw things, always aiming for each other's heads. What I threw left dents in the walls. I flipped over tables. He threw plates of food at me. We were monsters to each other. Ray mixed his alcohol and drugs. I only used drugs, but my moods were as volatile and mercurial as his, and our relationship devolved into a narrative of name-calling, shaming, and throwing things. It was all about hurting each other.

Chaos. Blur. Twenty-one. I moved out. Got my first job. Cocktail waitress at Whisky a Go Go. Already thick-skinned, I could handle myself with customers who groped, who ran out on bills. Being in a dark club where everyone was drunk or high or both was familiar. I could buy my own food now. I had a car that Ray had gotten me in our first year together. I found a roommate. Got another job as a maid and a third job in a record store. I ate little white speed pills so I could keep going with three jobs, smoked pot, and drank Vicks NyQuil to fall asleep. Still exhausted. Still addicted. I couldn't see it then, but I can see it so clearly now: I was clawing my way out of the blur and chaos, and it was damn slow.

Drugs made me crazy. I didn't know how to have a relationship without them. I didn't know how to have sex without them. They'd been the center of my universe for such a long time that I didn't know who I was. Ray left Los Angeles. I moved to Topanga Canyon and met someone who would become one of my best friends, who helped me be a person. He wasn't a boyfriend but a friend, and I can't put the word *just* in front of *friend* because he was never "just a friend." He talked to me about politics as we watched Watergate together. He told me I was smart. He gave me phone numbers to call about jobs. I stopped doing speed. I couldn't afford cocaine anymore, and it was a good thing. I only smoked pot and not every day. I was grateful that I didn't even want to do LSD. It made me feel crazier than I already did.

I was shaky on the inside all of the time. I was always afraid. I didn't know how other people did life and looked so good, looked so happy. Then came the AA meetings and the therapists. Then came the great time of self-discovery, and the slow path to recovery and self-love.

She made it. Can you believe she made it? She clawed her way out to the top and tipped over onto the other side where she learned to become a person. It took so many years to learn to love her. It's now that I have the most overview and can pull her into my heart with tenderness. What she needed the most—and got the least of—was someone to love her. I'm sorry she was abandoned, once by my mother, once by me. *I won't leave you again*, I whisper to her when she dogs the edges of my dreams. She is my heroine, and I am hers. The addiction will always be there. Like a cancer in remission, it lies dormant at the feet of my younger self.

Women find a way. We all have a heroine who lives inside of us. We all have a story to tell. Telling our stories liberates us to love ourselves and command respect in the world. In all the great stories of transformation, the heroine makes a descent, which sets her upon a quest to find the gift, before she once again returns to the light. This was my descent, and it set me upon a path. . . .

~~~~~~~~~~~

For Reflection, Activity, and Journaling

We all have a time in our life—more likely several periods—where we meet suffering, regret, or fear. These times often reveal our greatest heroic impulses, while simultaneously remaining a carefully fenced-off area of our psyche. These are tough things to think about, let alone write about. Still, the writing of such stories can be liberating, instilling self-compassion where none was before.

This is not necessarily the writing that you share with others. The thoughtful process of mining the rawest and most painful of emotions can produce a sense of freedom from what has hurt us. These writings are sometimes meant to be shared. Other times they're best burned, perhaps in a ritual where you promise yourself that, like the phoenix rising from the ashes, strong and beautiful, you are no longer a prisoner of your past.

The exercise here is to write a letter to your younger self. However that letter might take shape, I hope you will include acknowledgment for the suffering and striving of your younger self, soothing from the older self to the younger self, and, most important, an overview of how things have worked out for you—or, at the very least, how they are still in process.

Here are some suggested questions/topics you can cover in your letter:

1. In what ways do you judge your younger self? When you think of her, do you think of her kindly, or with a cringe?

2. In what ways do you have compassion for your younger self? Do you forgive her for her mistakes?

3. Are you able to see the ways your younger self was courageous? Do you celebrate her goodness, her accomplishments, and her bravery?

4. What would you tell her now about how life—*her* life, your life—will work out for her?

PART TWO:

CREATRIX RISING

While midlife men grow into silver-haired foxes, women at midlife are the target of anti-aging messages. Think about it. "Anti" means *against*, therefore "anti-aging" literally means *against aging*. We'd be shocked to see *anti* in front of *Black*, *Latino*, or *gay*, turning them into words that would then be ugly and bigoted. Yet somehow, *anti-aging* slips through the cracks as one of the last great bastions of incorrectness, acceptable to the majority of the culture.

Many women are still struggling to make peace with the aging process. We're doing so in the face of an advertising culture that on the one hand tells us to just be ourselves and recognize our strength, while on the other tells us we are only desirable with smooth, unlined skin and firm thighs, not to mention hair that is bereft of any gray.

I applaud the spontaneous uprising that is taking place on social media, clearly a Creatrix kind of move. All over Facebook and Instagram, I see midlife women posting pictures with statements that proclaim a newfound beauty and vitality that comes with age. Women who are proud of their silver hair. Women who are pursuing their art. Women who refuse to let anyone else define who and what they are. These women know the secret, that celebrating life to its fullest—without shame or apology for one wrinkle, one more year, or one silver hair—is key to self-empowerment.

The same message we've given our daughters, grand-daughters, and nieces about finding their voice and standing in the light of their truth has reached our own hearts when it comes to aging. Instead of lamenting the passing of youth, midlife women are laying claim to the rich and textured beauty of our years, where age is seen as an asset instead of a catastrophe.

How would we ever have applied the notion of anti-aging to someone like Ruth Bader Ginsburg? What I think of when I remember Justice Ginsburg is her work ethic, her tenacity, her strength, and how she fought for the rights of all of us. I think of her passion for opera. I'm enlightened by her ability to make and keep unlikely friends with whom she managed to find common ground. I'm inspired to want to become like her as I grow older, because of the qualities of heart that she demonstrated that can only come with age.

Or what about Carole King, whose Hyde Park concert in London, the summer of 2016, was nothing less than spectacu-lar? I've watched that concert several times, and the part that always gets me is when Carole is singing "(You Make Me Feel Like A) Natural Woman." Behind her is a huge screen showing her singing the same song when she was twenty-eight, the older Carole King and the younger harmonizing with each other. That's what we learn to do when we hit midlife: we start harmonizing with our younger selves. There is a nobility to that, a great, sacred arc of a woman's life. "Anti-aging" is an ageist message that damages us as it proclaims youth to be the only desirable state for a woman.

Back to the women on social media. Their message opens us to new possibilities, although it's important to note that the message that midlife and older years are a powerful passage did not happen overnight. This message has been centuries in the making, but in the last century in particular the message has sped up. Women were given the vote. Women joined the workforce. Oral birth control and the ability to control family size changed everything. Colleges and universities that were once the purview of males opened to women. We began the arduous climb of upward mobility and acknowledgment in the workplace. And in recent years, a light shining into dark and ugly corners of the culture liberated us further, as seen in the #MeToo movement. All of this has contributed to our growing up, seizing the fruits of our third act with pride. We have become elders whose hard-won wisdom is paving the way for the next generation.

This is the Creatrix rising, and we are her.

Chapter Five

Menopause,
the Spiritual Bridge

M enopause announced itself with a series of unpredictable and unwelcome changes. I began having hot flashes. I've met women who tell me they think they're having hot flashes, but they're not sure. A hot flash is sort of like an orgasm: you definitely know when you're having one!

My hot flashes would wake me from a sound sleep in the middle of the night, a core of heat radiating from the center of my body and spreading like lava on a hillside. Not all were that dramatic, but at the very least, my hot flashes felt as if I'd been locked in a sauna for too long. Sometimes I would get out of bed and stand on the deck, letting the cold of the Rocky Mountain winter engulf me. Of course, those were in the winter months. In summer, I had little recourse but to drench myself with water from a spray bottle that I kept on my nightstand and hope that the evaporation would cool me down. As one of my girlfriends told me, menopause is like a glowing sweat that lasts for years.

It wasn't just the nights; it was the days, too. Without warning, the core of heat would begin to spread at the most inopportune times. At the office, in a restaurant, a store, a library—you name it, I probably had a hot flash there. I learned to dress in layers, so that I could remove clothing when the heat hit. I drank iced water and dabbed my forehead with paper towels from the ladies' room. Sometimes I would have intense hot flashes in quick succession, and other times I would slowly glow. The new normal of being in my fifties was a baptism by fire.

My periods stopped. I had a sense of being in the throes of an identity crisis. *Menopause.* It was such a big word, and it had so much baggage attached to it. It was also a force, a physical and emotional force that was ushering me toward the threshold of something new. Who was I? A midlife woman? An old woman? An aging woman? As the process progressed, I felt myself fall into grief. At a time when I was struggling to understand what this life change meant, I could not articulate the profundity of the passage but only whimper that I feared losing my sexuality and femininity.

I'm of a generation that whispered about women's blood in hushed and often shameful tones. According to my sixth-grade sex education class, menstruation was a matter of strange new hygiene requirements. My mother told me that what was happening to me was a celebration of becoming a woman while simultaneously cautioning that I could now become pregnant. I wasn't sure what becoming a woman was about. I had cramps, and I was embarrassed by the bulky and uncomfortable Kotex pads that were part of this new regimen. But mostly, what I needed as a young girl was for someone to fit the pieces together, to explain to me the significance of the physical changes. The talk about biology was so sterile. Was this why there was a kind of secretiveness around having a period that was tinged with shame?

It's only as I recall the experience of being young and having periods that I can see how comforting it would have been for someone to suggest that the body's monthly blood was the physical manifestation of creativity. The body, *my* body, could now make children. The passage of blood didn't make me a woman, but it escorted me into becoming a woman. I could have benefited from knowing that having a period could be a touchstone, a monthly reminder that I was the keeper of life, creation, insight, and light, all of which would support me in the motherhood phase until that rich fertile river dried up. And while that's true reproductively, it does not apply either creatively or spiritually.

Menopause pulled me to the peak of observation, where I viewed the last vestiges of a youth that would no longer be. Like a lot of women, I had only ever seen my periods as an inconvenience. But when they stopped and the blood dried up, I was left with grief. Blood bookends a large section of a woman's life. There are the years of having periods and the years of the periods stopping. What came before the blood was childhood innocence. What comes after the blood stops? Are we being born into a new life with creative vision, or do we buy the worn-out stereotype of being old and used up? The choice is attitudinal.

Throughout the years, I made choices, both good and bad. In terms of the good, I spent a fair amount of time in therapy and a lot of time reading the Christian mystics. I also read the great Sufi poets and began to relate to a human longing that seeks to know its home. I made a decision to live the examined life. This manifested itself in the study and practice of meditation and quiet reflection in the early morning hours, a single flame from a candle lighting my way. As I grew in my understanding of myself, I was coaxed by a longing to spend time in nature. Nature reflects cycles and changes that we experience in our own bodies. She comforts us when we grow still in her.

When confronted by the passage of menopause, I didn't realize I was embarking upon a path of awakening. I see that time now in retrospect, and just like I wished I could have had conversations when I was first having periods, conversations in menopause would have been useful, too. While the great wise woman who could have imparted such things never showed up, my husband addressed the psychic and physical discomfort I was experiencing, and that turned things around for me. An insightful and thoughtful man, he challenged me to explore the roller coaster of emotional and physical symptoms, reframing them into what he called "an essential process into a new and greater creativity."

His words spoke to a truth that I knew but hadn't considered, which is that creativity does not come from the pretty places in our lives. Gestation does not happen in sunshine. Creativity is often born from darkness, mud, and chaos.

As I explored this new possibility, I found that just like the surge of heat from hot flashes, a surge of creativity was rising up in me, the roots of which were in menopause. The desire to make something came at me with an urgency, as well as a newfound allegiance to my deepest passion.

I took my husband's overview to heart, and as a result, the passage of menopause had captured my imagination. I was on a path to exploring who I was becoming. It's only now, in my late sixties, that I understand how menopause doesn't just bring about physical changes, but is a spiritual bridge from one phase of a woman's life into another.

Robert Graves named the culmination of a woman's older years the Crone. But crones are used up and considered ugly, and their image is a cultural projection of fear onto women. The name Crone deserves to be discarded.

There are certain words in the culture that we should never try to revive because of the ugly baggage they carry. For example, the N-word will never deserve resurrection as something painted in a positive light because the root of the word was meant to demean, just as the word *crone* is meant to insult.

The reason that the word *crone* should be replaced is because its etymology and meaning pose the question: What good is a woman who cannot bear children? And further: What good is a woman without youthful beauty? The menopausal woman, the Crone, is not desirable. Because of those questions, we midlife and older women have been wrapping ourselves in the myth of insignificance. We tend to grieve the passing of youth instead of claiming and celebrating the beauty and power of maturity.

What I learned by traversing the path of menopause is that menopause is a great spiritual awakening, filled with the rich, dark mud of creativity. The myth of insignificance is not the truth, and all around us we see women rising above those worn-out attitudes, creating new, more beneficial attitudes in their wake.

My overview of a woman's journey is not unique or special. We live in a time when we are witnessing the consciousness of women expanding. We are celebrating ourselves, claiming our voices, embracing our years, and growing in our wisdom. You don't have to look very far on social media to see that there are hundreds of groups welcoming women who are letting their hair go silver, welcoming women who celebrate the passage of midlife. And there are those women who post individual pictures, proud of the wisdom of self-acceptance. It is those women who demonstrate the courage to come forward and claim their authentic experience, who are on the cutting edge of this emergence. They are replacing the Crone and becoming the Creatrix.

For Reflection, Activity, and Journaling

Menopause can be seen as more than just uncomfortable symptoms. This female passage can be seen as a baptism of fire and water. The hot flashes are the fire, and the water is the sweats. Underneath every physical symptom in life is a feeling. Emotions, especially the way they're connected to women, have long been held as an indicator that something is wrong or out of balance. But a woman who cries or rages during menopause may have good reason for tears and anger. Emotions are signposts as to where we are in our journey. They are what textures our heart, pulling us toward greater self-knowledge.

The Creatrix is defined as a woman who makes things, and the purpose of making things can give new form to tears and anger, to create something new. Emotion is the fodder and fertilizer for the garden of creativity that is birthed in menopause.

1. If you have hot flashes or night sweats, what are the emotions under those physical sensations? Do you feel weepy? Angry? Off-balance? Is there a story that goes with the emotions?

2. Try this: Take the physical event and sensation of hot flashes or night sweats and assign a symbol to it. For instance, how is a hot flash like a burning desire to do something different in your life? Can a hot flash be seen as a burning devotion or commitment to something? While the physical symptoms of menopause are part and parcel of the transition, gleaning the spiritual or psychological symbolism and metaphor is more of a choice. What is the story around, for instance, the burning desire or burning commitment?

CHAPTER SIX

THE FORESHADOWING

I woke up with my stomach in knots. I still couldn't believe the country had elected a man who said men could do anything they wanted to women if they were a celebrity—"Grab 'em by the pussy," he'd said. And that the Evangelical Christians, who'd always held themselves up as the pinnacle of American morality, thought this man was sent by God. Former Minnesota congresswoman Michele Bachmann had faced the cameras after the *Access Hollywood* tape came out, and waved her hand in the air, assuring everyone it was all just "boy talk." Whatever the hell that means. In the marrow of my bones, I could feel how much this new president disrespected women, and it sickened me.

But today was a new day, and along with a lot of other people in the country, I was trying to talk myself into believing it was all going to be okay. We'd survive. Trump had won the election, and whether I liked it or not, he was the president. Something I'd heard a long time ago popped into my head: This being so, how shall I proceed?

My husband pointed out a newspaper article about a women's march a few days before the event. It was a small column. It said the marchers were meeting at the library on Main Street and marching into Lithia Park. We were living in Ashland, Oregon, at the time.

"I'm gonna go," I told him. "I want to do something." The paper said that city officials were anticipating six hundred people. That seemed like a good number, given that Ashland only had a population of about twenty thousand.

So on January 21, 2017, with a camera around my neck and my phone in my back pocket, I made my way into town early. When I got there, Main Street was already jammed with people. Women were wearing knitted pink hats with cat ears—"pussy hats." That made me smile. They must have known about the march long before I did, because these were all knitted by hand, each one slightly different in shape and color, depending on its maker. I found myself loving all the women who'd sat down with yarn and knitting needles to make something that so aptly represented the tone of the day, one that proclaimed: We shall not be humiliated or kicked down. Humor has a way of holding the facts up to the light, allowing for clarity.

The crowd was diverse—women my age and older, mothers, daughters, friends. And there were husbands, sons, fathers, and boyfriends. It sure looked like a lot more than six hundred people to me, but then I wasn't really sure what six hundred people looked like.

On that crisp January morning, the police department had blocked off Main Street, and as I crossed to get to the library, where the protesters were gathering, I went by a solitary cop who was directing people and answering questions.

"Hey, thanks for being out here," I said to him.

"My pleasure." He smiled.

"Do you need anything?" I asked him.

"I could use a cup of coffee."

"How do you take it?"

"Black," he answered.

"Give me a second. I'll be right back."

Instead of going to the library, I went to Bloomsbury Books, where there is a coffee shop upstairs. I was smiling at the irony—how many times in my life I'd brought a man coffee. But this time, it was a gift, not the result of an expectation. At the top of the stairs, dozens of women were waiting in line, the coffee shop being one of the few places on Main Street that was open that morning. After placing my order for black coffee, I took the lens cap off my camera and walked over to a table of about eight women, all wearing pussy hats. "Can I take your picture?" I asked them. "I want to remember today."

"Sure. Let us take yours, too." It was as if we were all old friends. A spirit of unity filled the air. I took pictures, commented on their hats, and laughed about how the growing crowd looked like much more than six hundred people. Then one of them took a picture of me with the group, with my camera. Just before she pushed the shutter, she took off her hat and handed it to me. I wore it with pride for the few seconds it took her to snap the picture. I love that photo. I don't know a single name of anyone in that group of women, and I don't remember if we even introduced ourselves. We didn't have to. We all knew who each other was: women wearing pussy hats and looking straight into the camera, smiling the smile of fierce determination.

When my coffee order was up, I thanked the women and we said our goodbyes, and I walked back across the street to the cop. He'd forgotten in the throes of the chilly morning and the growing crowd that he'd wanted coffee.

"You're a sweetie," he said.

"You, too. Have a good day." That was the end of that. Bringing him coffee was as much a part of the swelling feeling of goodwill and hope as anything I witnessed that day. We were all going to be there for each other, I knew it.

At the library, I took more pictures. I listened to someone talk about the power of the collective voice. The mayor said something about everyone being there—maybe he thanked us, I don't recall. Then we were off, marching down Main Street to Lithia Park. At the corner of the first block, I found my friend Taffy in front of a real estate office and fell into step with her. As our eyes drank in the people, the signs, the mood, we kept saying over and over, "Can you believe this?"

Hand-painted signs. Hand-stenciled signs. Some neat and some raw. A grandmother walking with a daughter and granddaughter stopped when I asked if I could take their picture. Grandmother held a carefully made sign:

> WE WELCOME: ALL RACES
>   ALL RELIGIONS
>   ALL COUNTRIES OF ORIGIN
>   ALL SEXUAL ORIENTATIONS
>   ALL GENDERS
> WE STAND WITH YOU. YOU ARE SAFE HERE.

Another woman half my age proudly held a sign above her head: WOMEN RISE UP!

More signs. Families with strollers and young children. Daddy sporting a sign for the family: PROTEST IS PATRIOTIC. Someone had a sign that read: BUILD BRIDGES, NOT WALLS. Another: DON'T MOURN. ORGANIZE! That one was the last photograph I took. Then I just let myself walk and take it all in. An atmosphere of welcoming, of fierce love and connection, rumbled under the soles of hundreds upon hundreds of boots and athletic shoes walking along Main Street.

When I finally made it to Lithia Park with Taffy and her husband, Ross, who'd joined us, I stood with them on a hill and watched the rest of the marchers fill the park. Wave after wave after wave. This was not six hundred people. This was thousands of people, marching. I snapped pictures with my phone and loaded them up to Instagram, where I saw my nephew David's posts. For a few minutes, we went back and forth, sharing a story. He was marching in Denver, I was marching in Ashland, and we were with each other. I knew I was in the midst of a historic event, and I felt great about it.

I couldn't help but look further back when I thought of the 2017 Women's March. I wanted to know what got us to the march in the first place. What I saw was that the march of 2017 is still going on, as though a continuation of each time women marched together for a place of equality in the world. After the 2017 experience, I began to see that women everywhere were finding and expressing a beautiful, resounding voice that was the timbre of our salvation. Older women like me had the experience of an earlier feminism. Younger women carried the torch of new inspiration and vision. We'd been walking side by side for longer than any of us had realized.

◆ ◆ ◆

It was 1969 when I first heard about oral birth control—"the pill." It made life simpler. The idea that you could have sex and not worry about pregnancy being an unwanted outcome was appealing on many levels. Women could plan their families. This eased the financial pressures that often accompanies surprise babies. It also gave women a chance to manage their work life and career. And it gave women a chance to just enjoy the pleasure of sex. Without oral birth control, what became known as the sexual revolution might never have happened.

Though the pill was convenient, that convenience had unexpected consequences that revealed a darker side of oral contraception, proving it to be a double-edged sword. On the one hand, birth control pills liberated women. On the other hand, the pills also ensnared them. As feminism and the sexual revolution unfolded, not all men saw liberated women as sovereign souls but rather as a convenience for their own desires. The mindset of some misguided men was that women, now set up with oral contraception, should be ready for sex anytime and should want sex whenever they did. The result was women who weren't ready for all that sex but betrayed their better judgment so as not to be seen as "uptight"—the buzzword for those of us who did not completely embrace all sex, all the time. Birth control, and its effect on women and the culture, changed the game board, and it would take decades to sort out, even though it did move us forward.

In my lifetime, I've seen women rise to the top of companies, a position once the purview of men, though the wage gap between men's rate of pay and women's remains an issue. Each time a woman became a supervisor, a manager, a CFO or CEO, the women in her community rose, too. We made strides. We made inroads. All of it culminated in a greater hope for daughters, nieces, and granddaughters. This was the very beginning of what led us to assemble that day to march.

Though we were rising, we were also keeping secrets. As women climbed through the ranks to garner higher positions on the rungs of corporate ladders, we mostly kept to ourselves what we all knew to be true, which was that some men in business (not all) tried to tie our ascent to sexual favors. Or some men, made insecure by the women gaining on his own ascent in a company, would harass her verbally and, many times, physically.

Shortly after the 2017 Women's March, a loud crash of past and present colliding would be heard. The unresolved residue of the sexual revolution and the secrets that we kept ran head-on into each other. The last hill to climb before the smoke cleared again was the #MeToo movement. The antiquated idea that was an unfortunate tentacle of those early days of oral contraception, the notion that a woman should be ready to have sex with anyone at any time, had finally exploded.

It was not all men that caused this collision. And it was not all women. New ideas and change move awkwardly into our psyches, let alone the greater culture. A man like Harvey Weinstein, the film producer convicted of criminal sexual assault, brought the collision into focus. The collective secret of sexual harassment began to reveal itself in the stories we shared. The phrase #MeToo literally meant *me, too.* Too many of us had met Harvey Weinstein in some form or another. We knew what it was to be overpowered, shamed, violated, or abused by this type of individual. As we shared our stories and our consoling, the baggage of the sexual revolution had finally been thrown off. Weinstein came to represent the world of male sexual entitlement that women had been battling since they'd entered the workforce in large numbers decades before.

In the early 1980s, as I was trying to build a career of my own, I was working for a young executive who seemed to really appreciate me. I thought my hard work was finally going to pay off and I would shed my role of executive secretary and rise into management. I can't offer many details of the harassment I experienced because of a nondisclosure document I signed decades ago. So I won't name the company, or the man, or the other players who tried to protect him and his bad behavior.

I worked for someone whose insecurity and need for dominance over women manifested like this: He would call me into his office when there were other men present, and he'd ask me to take notes. Sometimes he even asked for my opinion. I was feeling pretty good about myself. And then one day, in front of a room full of men who also worked at the company, he asked me what I was doing that weekend.

"I don't know yet," I said. "I think I'll take a long bike ride, maybe go to a movie."

"A movie. That's great. Are you going to go with your boyfriend? You think he'll diddle you while you're watching the film?"

I didn't know what to say. My boss laughed. The other men laughed. I left the room to the sound of laughter, my face hot.

That kind of talk, mostly in front of other men, didn't let up. I grew to expect it. Sometimes I tried to laugh, just be one of the guys, but that only made me feel worse. I tried to get angry and tell my boss to fuck off, but the laughter would just grow louder, because part of the game was for him to get to me.

I thought it was my responsibility to find the right response to his inappropriate badgering, but of course, there is no right response. One day, I filed a complaint with the head of human resources, only to be chided by the woman in charge for not understanding that boys were just going to be boys.

From there, I took bold action and filed a lawsuit. I sued the company for creating and supporting a hostile work environment. Every coworker I'd ever considered to be a friend was now my enemy. And the worst of them, the most vocal, were other women. Couldn't I just let it go, they wanted to know? Didn't I know all men were like that?

My case settled before it ever got to court, and I was just one woman at the beginning of a line that would slowly make its way into a future of women breaking their silence, learning to support other women, and finally healing the shame, degradation, and humiliation caused by men like the one I once worked for.

I like to believe it was the combination of the #MeToo movement and the fresh courage of the 2017 Women's March that resulted in the 2018 midterm elections, when more women over the age of fifty ran for local, state, and national public office than had ever done so before in our history. Women were rising in protest, in consciousness, and in courage. The Creatrix was emerging and staking her claim.

~~~~~~~~~~~~~

For Reflection, Activity, and Journaling

It's been said that women need friendships more than men do. I don't know if that's true, but I do know that having women friends has enriched my life experience. Here are some questions you can think or journal about to help you explore the value of your relationships with other women:

1. Do you have one friend, two friends, or a small circle of friends? Do you ever meet in groups of women—book group, hiking group, therapy group? Do you find that you are more or less comfortable in groups of women as opposed to just being by yourself? Think of a time when you last met with a group of women, and make a list of what was special about it, or what you didn't like about it.

2. What women in your life have been the most supportive and encouraging of you? Family members? Women at work? Women you know socially? To whom do you turn when you seek support? What are the qualities of a person you turn to that make you feel safe and encouraged?

3. Think of a woman in your life who helped you to be stronger and more confident. How did she do that, and how did that change your life?

Chapter Seven

A Good Thing or a Bad Thing?

Finding your voice is a phrase most self-aware women are familiar with. The Creatrix has found her voice because she has spent a lifetime growing into her most authentic self. As a mature woman, she knows what she believes, what she stands for, and what she's willing to fight for. But learning what you stand for is a process that can be fraught with mistakes and misunderstanding.

Sometimes when you do something for the first time, you get it dreadfully wrong. That's what happened to me when I started my first and only women's group. I couldn't quite articulate what it was I really wanted at the time. I was afraid to say out loud that it had been decades since I'd been with a group of women with whom I shared my longings of love and life. I was hungry for the kind of emotional intimacy that comes from deep, caring relationships. And most of all, after years of applying myself to almost nothing other than work and marriage, I felt lonely, like I was always on the outside and looking in. I didn't know that what I was looking for was my own voice.

I hadn't always felt that way. In my early twenties, I lived in Los Angeles, where I became friends with a group of women I worked alongside in the entertainment industry. One of the things so special about the group was that we had each other's backs. Navigating the chaotic and unstable freelancing environment in the world of television often made me feel as if I were on my last job, and when that job was over, I'd never work again. Well, that and the fact that I had pretty horrible secretarial skills, which were a big requirement of the work I performed. But that group of women always kept me working. We all did that for each other. We'd call to let one another know about jobs that were coming up. We had contact names and insights that we shared. More than once, friends, even the ones who knew how awful my typing and spelling skills were, told me to use their name, and that's what got me the job.

In addition to making sure that everyone was getting the necessary work to pay their rent, we often met. Several of us would go out to dinner. There were celebrations and, in 1970s Los Angeles, always a ton of rock 'n' roll shows, replete with guest passes and good seats. Just one of the perks of the business in which we all worked.

During those years, we shared dreams and heartbreaks. There was never any doubt that we loved each other. Some of those wonderful times were the result of being twenty-something, unmarried, and without kids or other obligations. And some of it was just what happens to young women who are supported by friends as they try to figure out who they are and who they want to be in the world. That kind of love and having someone watch out for you was, I think, what I wanted to re-create. But, as the old saying goes, you can't ever go back.

I left Los Angeles in 1989 and moved to Boulder, Colorado. That move benefited me greatly. But I didn't realize how much I'd miss the camaraderie and caring I'd had with my L.A. group of women who were such a beautiful part of my life. I never forgot those friendships, and I never will. It was a special time.

Thirty years later, while edging up to the threshold of my sixtieth year, I had an idea about forming a women's group. I'd just finished reading *Divine Secrets of the Ya-Ya Sisterhood*, a novel about a group of women who forged deep, meaningful relationships and helped each other grow into better human beings. The book underscored my feelings of being off-center because I didn't have a nourishing circle of close women friends, and it inspired me to consider I could create that again. Of course, real life is never quite as perfect as what is portrayed in a novel or a movie. In real life, things are messy, and we have many more issues and complexities than fiction can possibly convey.

Nonetheless, I became a woman on a mission. I wrote in my notebook for a number of days about whom to invite and what topics and themes we could explore. I found a space in a converted barn for the first few meetings. I set a date and emailed invitations.

When the evening of the first meeting came, I set up a circle of cushions on the floor and brought cold bottled water for the table. I was excited. I was prepared. With my outline of what I wanted the first meeting to look like committed to memory, I called the meeting to order.

The outline was probably my first mistake. I thought I was creating a form within which we could work, but many of the women, as I later learned, were uncomfortable with what I considered to be the form. For them, "form" meant "too many rules." Not long after I was let in on that secret, things started to go downhill.

Instead of growing closer to the group that had settled into about eight to ten women, I felt awkward and self-conscious. Behind my back, women were complaining. Additionally, a power struggle between another woman and myself went from a simmer to a boil. I was torn between her vision for the group and my own. Eventually, this led to one of those flaming email exchanges we've probably all experienced, copied to everyone. We each committed to words of accusation, blame, and shame, and people took sides. I just wasn't prepared for the fallout. I left the group, feeling like everyone hated me, and shortly thereafter, the group fell apart.

Tears, disappointment, and a profound sense of hurt and failure dogged me for months. Some of it was knowing that I was, in part, to blame. I sought consolation in the writings of a Buddhist nun named Pema Chödrön. I often turned to her wisdom, looking for healing and a way forward. I pulled a book of hers down from the shelf and lost myself in it. The book was *When Things Fall Apart: Heart Advice for Difficult Times*. The title seemed like something that might make me feel better. Here's what she wrote that began to lift the pain of my failure: "When a thing happens, you don't always know if it's a good thing or a bad thing."

I'd judged what had happened with the women's group as a bad thing, and I was unrelentingly hard on myself about it. But the truth is, what happened turned out to be a good thing. It just took me time to see it. I was never going to be able to re-create the circle of women friends from my twenties. Those times belonged to a past Maiden archetype. I would always cherish the special passage that I'd had with those women in Los Angeles. My disappointment slowly began to dissolve. This was an invitation to find the greater lesson of the experience.

But the desire to create a circle of women was only the surface request from my psyche. If I sat with myself quietly and didn't push away the discomfort, I could hear something that spoke to me beyond the pain. What emerged was a truer, brighter vision to stand in my own power and find my own voice. The experience with the women's group was the beginning of that quest, the doorway I stood at, soon to open and usher me into becoming a sixty-year-old woman.

I began a period of intense self-inquiry. I asked myself what sixty would be like for me. How did I see myself in that new decade? Who would I be as an older woman?

I hadn't shared my truth with those women, which was that I'd started the group because I was dogged by an existential loneliness, and that I was longing for female friendships that might help me make sense of where I was in life. I hadn't shared with them that at the edge of sixty, I was grieving the loss of my youth. My face was changing. My body was changing, and I wondered if I was now entering old age. Most of all, I didn't ask the questions that, in looking back, I think deserved to be answered: What did I *really* want from these other women, from a group like this? And, more important, what did *they* want? All of that amounted to my being in the way, as opposed to being someone who could open a door.

I learned that speaking my truth is important, but strangely, it became more difficult after the group fell apart. Clearly, I'd learned something, but my physical voice changed, and I experienced a strange phenomenon whenever I had to speak to any sort of group or gathering. Over the next several years, I found it more and more difficult to talk in front of even a small gathering of people. At first I just had a rapid heartbeat and sweating, but as time went on, the symptoms changed to my throat literally shutting down. As I tried to speak out loud in front of a group, it was as if I were being strangled. Instead of my normal voice, what came out of me was something thin and stretched into a high pitch with little volume. Worse, as much as I pep-talked myself or tried to breathe deeply, I had no control over losing my voice.

We've all had bad dreams where someone's chasing after us and we're scared, but when we try to scream for help, barely a whisper comes out. That's what it was like.

In the beginning of this new voice problem, which lasted a few years, I could sometimes push through it, and after a minute or so, my real voice would return. After a while, though, I couldn't even push through it, and I just sounded like a woman being strangled.

What was so odd about losing my voice (literally) is that my personality is fairly outgoing, and I generally like people, so I didn't understand what was really happening to me. Why could I be fine one minute and then in the next, when giving a simple introduction to a group of twenty or so, experience not having a voice? The issue of speaking my truth became a much bigger calling than I'd initially imagined.

The twenty-twenty hindsight provided by the intervening years gave me some clarity. I was in the process of leaving my old self behind and beginning to grow into the new self that is an embodiment of the Creatrix archetype. But my voice was new, yet unformed, even as the old voice still tried to come out but no longer could.

I'd felt painfully judged by the women with whom I had tried to form a group. Facing my own role in the failure of my creation was painful, too. I'd made plans and envisioned the way I hoped things would unfold, and none of it happened. That my failure had been so public was both humbling and humiliating. But life has a way of pushing us forward in spite of our shortcomings.

As the doorway to my sixties opened, I felt a little bit crazy. I didn't have a voice, and I wondered if one might ever return.

For Reflection, Activity, and Journaling

The changes that come upon us as we enter midlife sometimes bring fear and anxiety. That universally human question that dogged us in our teens and twenties—"Who am I?"—is back. Even though our hearts feel young, we are no longer young. What do we do with the changes?

Here are some questions to help you explore this:

1. Do you wish you had more emotional intimacy in your friendships? Why do we need that so much? How do we find our people, our tribe?

2. What have been your most spectacular failures in life? What weren't you seeing at the time? What do you see about yourself now?

3. Have you noticed times when your voice is strong and other times when you don't seem to have one? I sometimes think of what I wish I'd said twenty minutes after the fact. Where did my confidence to speak up go? What is it that gets in the way of speaking your truth and feeling good about it? Are you afraid of being judged? Are you afraid you'll be wrong? What keeps you from speaking up?

Chapter Eight

Finding Voice, and Belonging:

A Story of Reinvention

Ashland, Oregon, is a little town nestled in the Rogue Valley, a place that feels like it's sitting snug and secure in the palm of a hand. Two squat mountain ranges rise up on either side of green cedar forest and old fruit orchards, just high enough to shelter the dale that is home to the Oregon Shakespeare Festival and a half-dozen wineries. I lived in Ashland for only four years, but in that time I began to grow into the person I always believed I could become.

My husband, Dean, and I moved from Boulder, Colorado, to Ashland in the summer of 2014, unaware we weren't quite the small-town people we hoped we might be. While Dean settled into his consulting work, I settled into living a lifelong dream of becoming a writer. Our days were slow and deliberate—nothing like the frenetic work schedule we'd left behind in Colorado. Time was suddenly abundant, and we took advantage of unstructured days to hike the woods around Ashland and make the short drive to lakes that welcomed us with the grace of their serenity.

For the first time in my adult life, I did not go to a job every day. Instead, I got up in the morning and wrote. It might be a more apt description to say that what I did every morning was to practice writing. I ventured outside of Ashland to attend writing workshops, learning about writing from amazing teachers who challenged, criticized, and praised my efforts.

I was in the process of reinventing myself, imagining myself as a new person, and this new person had things to say and was armed with pen and notebook. I got my first paid writing job in Ashland at a little newspaper called *The Rogue Valley Messenger*. I wrote lifestyle pieces, interviews with interesting people who either lived in the valley or were visiting. One week I'd be interviewing a local documentary filmmaker, and the next I'd be interviewing the valley's number one burlesque dancer. I delighted in seeing my name appear in a byline on a regular basis, and the small checks that followed were sweet signs of acceptance.

Still, the challenge of expressing myself through speaking persisted. Even with my newly claimed passion and the accompanying validation, whenever I shared my thoughts or opinions with a group of people, my voice continued to sound like a strangled cat. The physical sensation of succumbing to the vise in my throat was something I feared would never end. No amount of deep breathing, meditation, or positive self-talk could undo the garrote that tightened around my words, it seemed—until I met a poet who healed my affliction.

Richard Blanco was Barack Obama's inaugural poet and spoke at the president's second inauguration. He is the author of a dozen books of poetry and a couple of memoirs. On the day that he stood in front of the inaugural crowd in Washington, D.C., to read his poem "One Today," he was following in the footsteps of Robert Frost and Maya Angelou, among others. The first Latino to be given that honor and the first gay man, he recited his poem about unification, describing an America that had her arms and her heart open wide.

In the early spring, I got a call from my editor at *The Messenger* asking me to interview Richard Blanco. The poet was coming to Oregon to conduct a class at Southern Oregon University for professors and high school teachers about teaching poetry. He would also be teaching a class on poetry at the high school, followed by a public reading. Giddy with the excitement of getting what felt like the best assignment ever, along with the insecurity of wondering whether I was really up to the task, I ordered two of Richard's books and began reading them, letting his words inform my interview preparation.

On the day of the interview, I called Richard's number at the time appointed, and did my best to act like a pro instead of an excited schoolgirl, even though that was how I felt on the inside. It was to be a phone interview, so I sat on the couch in my office, legs stretched out in front of me, laptop balanced on my thighs, headset plugged into my phone. I asked my first question and began typing his answers into the computer as we spoke. Every now and then, I would think, *Oh my God, I'm really interviewing Richard Blanco.*

The last question I asked him was "How do you define poetry?"

"Poetry is a revealing of the extraordinary within the ordinary," he answered. Then he told me a personal story to illustrate his point. He'd been sitting in his family's kitchen one day, watching his mother chop onions. He'd watched her do this thousands of times, but on that day, he saw his mother and the act of making dinner as something more. In this simple act, his mother was revealed to him as the very lifeblood of their family. She cared for them all in a deep and abiding way that encompassed his life and informed the man that he was . . . and he saw all of this in the chopping of onions for an evening meal.

"In that moment, I understood what poetry was," he told me.

Two weeks later, my interview appeared in *The Messenger*, and I drove to Southern Oregon University to sit in Richard's classroom, hoping to absorb the sensitive connection that he had to words, and to his placement of them into life and onto the page.

People who know me know that I have this weird emotional tic of always feeling like I've gotten off the bus at the wrong stop. So when I walked into the classroom, even though I recognized a few professors I'd met before, I felt they wouldn't want me to sit with them. I waved at them, and then my interloper self took a seat about eight rows back from the front. Tables were stretched three or four in length, with chairs on one side facing the lectern and the screen.

This was the first time I'd seen Richard in person. He walked to the lectern and began to address us. He was a warm, smart, and funny speaker, and I quickly fell under his spell. On the screen behind him, he projected old family photographs, the kind with scalloped edges and a white frame, photos taken in the 1970s, photos whose colors had faded into muted tones.

In one, an older woman is sitting next to the television, but not just any television—this TV is like a piece of furniture, the centerpiece of the room. In another photo, someone has pulled lawn chairs into the living room to accommodate overflowing guests. These are everyday images of an everyday life that, in an exercise he leads, we are asked to examine and describe.

The images hold clues about everything, including familial closeness, habitat, and time. A father who smiles proudly with his hand on the piece of television furniture. Richard's *abuela* (grandmother), surrounded by family members who clearly hold her in esteem. The exercise underscores the need for keen observation and feeling.

As I study the pictures, I begin to feel an old grief, a long-ing that's always asking and wanting to belong. The feeling plays right into my interloper self, who is now squirming in her chair. I have my own photo album running in my head, small moments of family, blurred from the lack of consistency. I want to push it away, get back to Richard's pictures on the screen, and then I see it: my mother, with her hand on a piece of furniture that is a television, not unlike the photo of Rich-ard's father. The memory moves me. Richard's father. My mother. Her pride of being able to bring such a thing into the house. And for me, that color television as a piece of furniture was a true prize. Lurking below the surface of my longing was the teardrop shape of a flawed mother who loved me, and I knew, in that moment, we'd once belonged to each other.

Old photographs. Old memories. Family. The tattered and worn edges of faded pictures and faded lives that reveal the struggle to find meaning and create belonging—this is a small moment of realization. I realize how Richard has taken his very definition of poetry and demonstrated it to the class.

Following the exercise, Richard puts up a poem about family on the screen. He reads the first stanza, and the images from the photographs start to come alive in the light and shapes he has woven into words. The stanza washes over me, and I'm feeling longing, hope, love, and grief, all at the same time. He asks for a volunteer to read the next stanza aloud. Without thinking, without feeling one erg of nervous energy, I offer to read the stanza.

In that moment, everything I'd ever learned about honor-ing poetry through the spoken word came rushing back to me. All those classes at Naropa University with Anne Waldman, Anselm Hollo, and Rick Fields—all those poetry readings I'd attended—came back to me in an instant. So when I read the stanza to the class, it was with a trusted cadence that revered the poet and his poetry. I only wanted to give the stanza its due.

When I'd finished reading, a woman sitting in the row in front of me turned around and gave me a look that said, "Well done." The flash of unexpected approval made me think maybe I hadn't gotten off the bus at the wrong stop. Maybe this was my belonging: giving myself to the art of wordsmiths, poets, and the feelings of weathered memory albums that were less than perfect, yet whole.

Something extraordinary happened to me as I delivered that poetic stanza to the room: I forgot about myself. I forgot to notice whether I felt judged or adequate. The poem simply deserved a voice. That old strangled cat voice was my voice when I wasn't deeply moved by anything, and it held sway over me until I was transformed by something amazing. I was done with that old voice and wanted to speak now from a profound truth. No longer a voice of me, personally—rather, a voice speaking from my greater, higher self.

It took some time for me to integrate what I'd learned, the conclusion being that my voice was freed up because the poem had become bigger and more important than I was. But back then, sitting in Richard's classroom at Southern Oregon University, I wondered: Could it be that simple? Could it be that when I spoke, I only had to give of myself, instead of thinking about how I was being seen, or whether or not I was doing it right?

I lingered for a moment with these questions while the class continued. When I got home, I knew that something had shifted. I'd just met my new voice, and she was the Creatrix, rising within me.

The next evening, I went to Richard's public reading at the local high school auditorium. As he spoke his poetry, I closed my eyes and lost myself in the brevity of words that conveyed so much emotion. I wept silently, giving in to the rapture of the experience. Richard read about a sense of belonging. It was an extension of what I'd experienced in his earlier class, an inkling that I did, in fact, belong to something. Was it to my mother and our complex relationship, now buffered by her death? Or was it that I belonged to wooded trails, to the small pack that was my husband and my dog? I belonged to quiet mornings and journal pages. I belonged to a sisterhood that I'd not quite found but held dear, nonetheless. I looked to the stage where Richard read so confidently. I aspired to be like him, to belong to a self with a voice that spoke truth, and was unafraid.

In the sorting out of that profound experience, I never made the time to tell Richard Blanco that his light illuminated my path to liberation, or that from that point forward, my voice came back to me. Not only could I write down the things that I needed and wanted to say, I could speak them to more than just one person without choking. In a picture of Richard's father resting his hand on the television that was furniture, in the memory of my mother buying us a similar kind of television and demonstrating a similar sense of pride—pride of ownership, pride of doing well, pride of the gift she was able to give us—I'd found a clear example of the extraordinary within the ordinary.

The poet inspired me and still does to this day. In his classroom I began to discover the voice of my Creatrix. She knows who she is and what she stands for, and where she belongs. She lives life as an artist, creatively and with passion. Seeing the extraordinary within the ordinary became a template for how to live life as if it were poetry.

For Reflection, Activity, and Journaling

For each of our personal stories, there is a turning point—an "out of the ashes, the phoenix rises" moment when we are pulled toward the resolve of either comedy or tragedy. This is often a time of reinvention. Reinvention awakens us again and again during the course of our years.

1. What is your "out of the ashes" story, a pivotal time when you seemed to crash and burn only to rise again like the phoenix? Was the resolve tragic or was it comedic? (*Comedy* doesn't necessarily mean "funny." It also means "a container for joy.")

2. What were the gifts of passion, wisdom, and vision that came out of your crash-and-burn journey?

3. What about that crash and burn gave you a different sense of yourself? What gave you the courage to grow?

4. Who did you receive help from in your life and who or what inspired you to live larger?

PART THREE:
EMBODYING THE CREATRIX

In my lifetime, I've witnessed a steady and accelerated evolution of women that begs the question: Is this a Darwinian moment?

When my mother approached older age, she told me that growing old was a terrible thing. For her generation, this was not an isolated attitude. America is a young country that values youth and sexiness above substance and depth. In her generation, how else was a midlife woman to feel but used up and disposable? The perception of the old crone has long been supported by advertising. If advertising only shows older women as feeble, frail, and unattractive, whether that's true or not, the attitude infects the culture, and we begin to take the images as truth. Worse, if advertising never shows an image of a woman over the age of forty-five or fifty, the unspoken message is that she is useless and invisible.

Is the way that our culture views older women uniquely American? In other countries, where they dance the tango up to the very end of life, mature women are not defeminized or desexualized the way they are here in America. Here, we tout anti-aging cures as if age were a disease, and women spend billions of dollars on keeping the face of youth for as long as possible, our identities and our creativity tied to some false form of beauty.

A friend who is about to turn forty told me a story that illustrates our biased American way of seeing older women. She and her husband were vacationing in Italy and had stopped at a shop across the street from a beach. Returning to their rental car, they found it wouldn't start, so they attempted to push it out of the parking space to roll downhill, where they'd seen a garage. As my friend's husband pushed on the car and she steered, a woman came running across the street from the beach to help. Appearing to be in her late sixties, the woman was wearing a bikini and sandals. She was tanned and lean, my friend told me, but her skin was crepey and her musculature ropey. A little bit of a belly sagged over the bikini bottom. Without any conversation, the woman placed her hands on the car next to my friend's husband and helped to push. Once the car was out of the parking spot and set to roll downhill, the woman ran back to the beach, with a quick wave.

"What was so striking about the incident," my friend said, "was the lack of self-consciousness this older woman had about being in her bikini. She ran to help with the same amount of strength and determination of a much younger woman, only she did it unabashedly, unashamed in her bikini."

Hearing the story, the word "unashamed" landed with a painful thud because I knew that here, in America, we shame women for growing older rather than revere them. A seventy-year-old woman publicly enjoying the sensual delights of the sunshine in a bikini would be a less likely scenario here than in other places in our world.

All over the planet, women like Angela Merkel, Theresa May, and Jacinda Adern are the heads of government. They've proven that women are strong leaders, yet Americans are not yet inspired to elect a female president, though I believe we're getting closer.

This brings me back to my feeling that a Darwinian moment is upon us as we collectively engage in acknowledging that a revolution of creativity, self-worth, and courage is taking place with women—especially older women, who are beginning to embody the emerging archetype of the Creatrix.

To embody the Creatrix is to learn her nature and her qualities. By nature, the Creatrix is a sovereign soul, a seeker, tapping into a higher vibration and consciousness that has always informed her, but now she loudly speaks and proclaims the truth of that higher octave. She weaves the qualities of creativity, courage, self-love, and acceptance along with the practice of gratitude into a pattern that is reshaping the collective consciousness of older women and how they are seen by the culture. Her strength comes from a knowing, a spiritual knowledge that she is the constant consciousness that is as old and wise as the universe. She no longer strives to prove herself through the trappings of youth but remains an uplifter to younger women.

Within this revolution of embodying the Creatrix as opposed to being defined by a society that has lost its way to wisdom and kindness, we cannot forget the Crone. The Crone is the Creatrix's shadow. The Creatrix represents the embracing of later years, an expansiveness of creativity and wisdom. The Crone represents bitterness, disdain of older age, a contraction into a sense of unfairness about irreplaceable youth. The turning point for life's third chapter as women reach out beyond motherhood is marked by the choice to model the Creatrix or the Crone.

The stories that follow are about women who carved out an empty space for the qualities of the Creatrix to emerge in their lives.

CHAPTER NINE

CREATRIX AS ARTIST

A ustin was her name, just like the city in Texas where I live today. She was my neighbor from the time I lived in Ashland. Her name was a symbolic foreshadowing of sorts, pointing toward the place where my husband and I would land after our time in Oregon. For this book, I tried to replace her name with something different for the sake of clarity, but it just felt wrong. Austin was Austin, and no one else.

Austin lived a short distance down the hill from me. By way of introduction, she left a handwritten invitation in my mailbox shortly after my husband and I had settled into our new home. "Please join me for wine and cheese," she wrote. "And meet some of your neighbors."

I don't think I've ever known anyone else who welcomed me with a handwritten invitation, so down the hill hubby and I trekked to meet Austin, as well as our other neighbors. The woman who greeted us and ushered us out onto her deck had snow-white hair and piercing blue eyes. Austin had been raised in the Florida Panhandle and spoke with a Southern lilt that immediately drew me in.

She offered us wine and lots of munchies. As I accepted a glass from her, I noticed a claw-foot bathtub sitting in the middle of her deck.

"Do you make bathtub gin?" I teased.

"No," she said with a smile. "I like to take a bath under the stars at night."

I looked more carefully at the tub. It was fully plumbed. "I thought I saw a hot tub on the other deck when we came in."

"Oh, the cover on that thing is just too heavy for me," she said. "I drained it."

The practicality and the whimsy of a claw-foot bathtub sitting on Austin's deck delighted me. As the evening progressed, I observed she also had a blue chandelier hanging from a tree limb in her garden. How could I not be curious about this woman? How could I not fall in love with her?

The walls of her living room were covered with masks she'd made. Some beautiful and some frightful, they were painted and adorned with beads, feathers, strips of leather, and ribbon. And there were paintings, canvases filled with color, each of them a story.

Austin was in her early eighties when I met her. Her creative spark and expression had not dimmed, only brightened with age. Her face was lined and wrinkled, of course, and there was something that shined through the physical appearance and encompassed a deeper beauty. My husband always said he thought Austin was stunning. Once a week, she filled her house with a younger generation of people that knew they were in the presence of a wise elder. Within this circle of young people, she drummed. They all drummed, a steady rhythm of calling in something greater, or maybe something lost.

There were so many things about Austin that I admired. From my sixty-four-year-old perspective, I wanted to be her in twenty years. She had been a psychotherapist in her younger days. When she retired from practice, she'd created an encore career as an artist. Although she made paintings, her masks were what I was most curious about. They were primitive and sophisticated all at once. And they reminded me of the different masks that we all wear throughout life, until we discover the beauty of what is underneath.

I'd only been in Ashland for a short time when I found out that Austin had a brain tumor. She came to our Christmas party that year, the belle of the ball, loved by everyone who met her. In spite of the tumor, she still walked every other day with Denise, the woman from across the street. Two souls huddled together, trudging up the hills to the trailhead, hanging on to one another for balance and for the love of it.

In her final year, Austin built a studio on her land with a door that opened up to the garden. There, in a last push of creative energy, she made the things for what would be her last art showing in Ashland. That was October. By the end of December, she was gone.

She had vowed that she would die in her living room because that room had the best light, and it was where her husband had died. I heard from a neighbor that Austin had moved into a hospital bed that had been placed in her living room. As the Christmas holidays approached, a young woman from the drumming circle hung lights over the deck railings so Austin could see them from where she rested. At one time, Austin told this young woman she'd never had outdoor Christmas lights before.

There was a family funeral, but for everyone else, there was a drumming circle on her deck attended by the generations of those who loved her.

When I think about the Creatrix emerging in this world in which women are ceasing to apologize for their age and are instead embracing their years, I think of my friend Austin.

Though I didn't know her well, she was an example for me of how I wanted to live my life. I believe that from an eternal place, she is trailing stardust behind her, as if to say, "This way . . . this way!"

For Reflection, Activity, and Journaling

As a little girl, I was an artist when it came to seeing the world in a free and wild sort of way. I lived barefoot, smudges of earth on my cheeks, braids and ponytails that wouldn't stay neat. I was wild, and life was wonderful. As an adult, I find myself looking for ways to get back to that time when I knew how to make homes for the sprites that lived under the tree, when the changing forms of clouds was a source of entertainment. On days that I live my best life, I live life in nature, and I live life as if all of it were art.

1. Consider keeping a nature journal where you can write about your experiences in the wild and what they teach you. Are there things you do to get in touch with and be connected to the wild part of yourself, the part that lives for the rapture of life's experience? Do you walk in nature? Do you contemplate the clouds or the trees?

2. A legacy journal of observations about your life can be done through poetry, prose, paint, photographs, or collage. You may find one of these formats compelling enough to try. Do you have a place to jot down your observations of life, a place to paint or draw?

CHAPTER TEN

CREATRIX AS HEALER

The kitchen at Shaffia's farmhouse has a wood-burning stove for heat tucked into a corner against a backdrop of old brick. Next to it is a love seat, the kind you sink into when you sit down and feel like the cushions are hugging you. The window over the sink looks out to a garden that bumps up to a vineyard, so that the tangled, growing green gives the illusion of stretching into infinity. The shelves under the wooden center island with a stainless-steel top overflow with bowls and plates of all sizes. Everything in her kitchen has a well-worn, well-loved feel to it.

From the first time I met her, Shaffia felt familiar to me, as if she were someone I'd known my whole life. Being with her is like receiving a special invitation. Her hands, her arms, her heart are wide open, as if to welcome you into the next moment and then the next. I imagine that anyone who comes to visit the farm leaves with the feeling that they are now part of Shaffia's family. That's how she was in the world, and it was a healing balm to legions of ailing souls.

Shaffia and I had met before I ever visited the farm. I knew her story because it was part of my husband Dean's story. When he was twenty-one years old, he took up residence with her. Their love affair was a great May/December romance—Dean was May and Shaffia December. Because of the age gap, the relationship only took them so far. Eventually the sorrowful unfairness of the age difference tore at the seams of their once love and stitched the jagged edges of what was left into a deep and caring friendship.

Life goes on, and Shaffia had other men in her life. Dean got married, got divorced, and then married me. The stuff of life intervened and changed the landscape of who they'd been to each other and how they were in the world now. Yet through it all, Dean stayed in touch with her and she with him.

I have to admit to being a little jealous of this woman my husband referred to as a "powerful healing force" in his life. "Powerful healing force" couldn't quite mask the bottom line for me: the fact that Shaffia was a former girlfriend.

Jealousy has little to do with someone else. It mostly has to do with oneself. Shaffia was never a threat. Rather, she was a story in Dean's history, a sweet and loving story in which love morphs and changes but survives nonetheless.

One Oregon summer's day, Dean and I made the drive from Ashland up the interstate to visit the healer, the ultimate Earth Mother, the Sufi dancer . . . all the things I envied, but I was going to try to make this work anyway. I did a lot of deep breathing on that drive, trying to lose myself in the vision of blue skies and green forest. Hills gave way to the flatland of ranches, farms, and miles of vineyards. In the late afternoon, our car crunched over the long gravel driveway as we made our way to a charming red farmhouse. In the distance I caught sight of a battered old battleship of a barn, surrounded by fruit trees and vegetable plots. Dean lowered one of the back windows of the car, and our dog Jeter perked up, sticking his head through the opening, his nose twitching with all the new information it was picking up.

Shaffia came out the back door of the house and stood at the edge of the walkway, waiting to greet us. She hugged Dean first, the kind of hug that speaks to decades of friendship and history. Then she hugged me, and I relaxed. Something about her, something about this place, made me feel at home.

That first visit was one of several during the time we lived in Oregon. I met Shaffia's daughter, granddaughter, and grandsons. I heard family stories and sat for hours on the back porch in the summer air, sharing meals and conversations, laughing and feeling like I was part of something. And Shaffia was always sweet with me, whether it was in sharing deep conversations or hanging out with a puzzle at the dining room table. I began to understand who she'd been in Dean's life, and how the man I loved came in part from her influence.

Dean reminisced about their early days together, how he'd played guitar for the Sufi dances they attended. I heard about the hammock stretched between the apple trees, the perfect place for napping. And I learned about how Shaffia had given the kind of praise and acknowledgment that was painfully missing from Dean's experience of his family of origin. It was the environment she created, the love and welcoming she gave so freely, that made Dean refer to her as a healing force in his life.

The name *Shaffia* was given to her by a Sufi in the late 1960s, and it stuck long after Sufi dances stopped being a thing for her. The meaning of the name is *mercy* or *pure healer*, and once I got to really know her, I thought the name described her well.

Shaffia is now approaching ninety, and with the accumulating years, she has receded to a place far away from where she used to be. She no longer remembers who was part of her life and who wasn't. She has no sense of how she welcomed and nourished and healed so many people who passed through her life. Alzheimer's has pulled her away from the world she once lived in, and we are all a little poorer for it.

Dean still stays in touch, though. One day, he called her on the phone, and she wasn't sure who he was. He called her by an old nickname, a silly, playful name— Bananas.

"How are you doing, Bananas?" he asked her. "Remember when you made pottery? Do you remember the piece you gave to me?"

The initial answers were hesitant noes. But as his gentle prodding and questions continued, she suddenly became animated. "Dean, Dean," she said. "You found me. I knew that you'd find me." I don't know where someone goes when they have Alzheimer's, but it is someplace new and far away.

I doubt that my friend Shaffia would have ever called herself a healer, though she clearly knew what healing was. I think that's why there were so many people who came to visit and stayed for longer than the meal. Once I saw Shaffia put her arm around her grown grandson as he sat sleeping on the couch next to the stove. She whispered to him, "Do you know how much I love you? Do you know how precious you are?" A faint smile came over his lips as he drank in her soft-spoken words.

No, Shaffia would not have called herself a healer, but she showed me what healing looked like in all its beauty. I began to see Shaffia, a woman for whom I'd once felt girlish jealousy, as a friend. She was a light in my husband's story and still loves purely and strongly, even as the tide is pulling her deeper into the sea. When I married Dean, Shaffia was part of the package. She became a healer in my life, too, a grande dame who raised six children and lost two of them to early deaths. She'd been a nurturer and supporter when

Dean as a young man needed someone to believe in him. In Shaffia, I saw the ultimate maturing of womanhood, a vision of the Creatrix with arms spread wide and a heart so big . . . there never was any overcrowding.

For Reflection, Activity, and Journaling

Consider what it means to be a healer in your life. The qualities of kindness and compassion may come to mind. There is also an energetic component, not something magical, but something born of encouragement and goodwill. Being a healer does not imply some kind of supernatural power; rather, it's a kind of gentle friendship, a relationship where you see the best in someone and open yourself to the best being seen in you.

Healing is something that we do for ourselves and for others, and it's ideal not to look for the results of healing experiences. Thinking that we know what the end result should be is not our business.

1. How have you given of yourself in a healing way?

2. Can you think of a time in your life when you experienced healing through the influence of another person? How did that come about?

Chapter Eleven

Creatrix as Teacher

In the fall of 1989, I was a determined girl-woman from Los Angeles who arrived at the doorway of a big, new adventure. I'd just become a student at Naropa University in Boulder, Colorado.

I was supposed to be starting at the University of Colorado, Boulder. That's where I'd applied and been accepted, but on the day I visited campus to create a class schedule, I was overwhelmed by the size of the sprawling campus in sprawling buildings that could barely tuck themselves into the edges of the Rocky Mountains in Boulder. Worse than the size was a personal sense of deep insecurity that somehow I would never make it in a school so large.

I was beyond the time in my life when I could simply play by the rules, do what I was supposed to do. As a younger student, I would have gone to college to meet people, to grow into an adult, to decide upon a career. But at thirty-six, I felt like I was breaking the rules just by walking through the door of a school like CU. The kids around me, all from good homes, looked like they'd beat me up and take my lunch.

After I got back to my apartment, I sat in my living room, panic breathing at the thought of being the student out of place in a sea of fresh, young faces. What I wanted was a shot of vodka to take the edge off the fear and self-doubt. Instead, I took a walk. I walked west, toward the mountains, up the busy street of Arapahoe Boulevard. I walked hard, determined not to cry. *What was I thinking, that I could go to college at my age?*

On my way home, I passed the campus of Naropa University. I only knew about Naropa because a guy I'd once dated in Los Angeles told me about it. In glowing terms, he told me it was a place where everyone meditated and was a vegetarian. In his eyes, those things made Naropa special. I wasn't up for being a vegetarian, but I was up for someplace off the beaten path where I might feel a little more at home.

In what used to be the Lincoln Elementary School, Naropa had taken up residence, using the old building for administration as well as some classrooms. Scattered around the grounds were cottages from the 1940s now used for classes, along with a new auditorium that had been built toward the back of the property—the largest building on the entire campus. Funky little Naropa, filled with its ideals and philosophy of Buddhism, sat gently in the shadows of the CU campus that loomed large on the hill above it. I walked into the administration building to ask for an application, and I never looked back.

Less than a month later, in the auditorium of soon-to-be fellow students, I was enjoying breakfast and the various speeches at orientation when a man sitting next to me whispered in my ear that I looked like I'd gotten off the bus at the wrong stop. It was true. But what he didn't know was that I'd been getting off at the wrong stop for years. This time, the wrong stop would turn out to be one of my better decisions.

I didn't have the look of the laid-back, casually attired students at Naropa. I was dressed in a short skirt and a crisp white blouse, more fitting for a job interview than a group meditation with students who mostly had come to major in Buddhist studies. And yes, group meditation was part of the orientation. In fact, meditation was woven into daily life at Naropa, and for me it was a welcome reprieve from my unrelenting mental state of self-judgment and occasional panic breathing.

The small institution was steeped in Buddhist traditions, courtesy of a heavily flawed but outstandingly brilliant Tibetan leader, Chögyam Trungpa Rinpoche. He had started the college in the mid-1970s, appealing to a generation of seekers who rejected a more conventional world. Naropa was clearly an alternative to what my generation had once referred to as "the establishment."

While I may have looked and even felt like the interloper, my education at Naropa would turn out to be perfect. I was in the right place at the right time in my life. My experience at Naropa continues to be one of the greatest, most positive influences in my adult life.

One teacher that I had during my first year was fired before my second year even started. For all its Buddhist kumbaya, Naropa was not exempt from the challenges and strains of institutional politics. I never knew why Susan Edwards was fired, only that it was painful for all of us who'd been her students.

The first class I had with this woman who would change my life was the Bible as Literature. She introduced me to the idea that biblical stories are metaphors containing rich symbolism, archetypes from another time that unfolded in the morality tales needed at that specific time in history. The class made me think in ways I'd never thought before. It was like my head was exploding from all the ideas and possibilities. Susan altered my perception of the world. I had a sense of thinking for myself, not just buying into what was told to me. That I could question beliefs and challenge myself to think critically about them was a new intellectual adventure for me.

Susan Edwards was an artist, a writer, a photographer, and a gardener. She pushed, challenged, and cajoled me to develop the strength of self-honesty. She saw the best in all her students, but she never praised my work unless I mined the depths of my psyche to produce it. She wanted all of us to think for ourselves and express that thinking in an articulate manner.

For the longest time, I believed Susan walked on water. When the second semester came around, I looked for any class of hers I could take. As a writing student with the major of writing and poetics, I could get credits I needed by taking her journaling class. Prepared to be challenged and inspired, I sat that first day at my desk in the circle she'd created. It was like her to set up her classroom where we could all see each other. She wasn't someone who stood at the head of the class, facing neat little rows while demanding conformity.

Journaling was a different kind of class. It was personal, not critical, and it required rigorous self-honesty. The writing prompts that Susan laid out during her lecture came so fast and furious that I couldn't keep up. My head was spinning. I looked at my class notes once I got home, and nothing made sense. How could there be so many things to write about? Surely she didn't mean for me to write about all of them? Besides, it would have been impossible, so I began to pick and choose what to write about, telling myself it was what she'd intended for us to do. No one could keep up with all those writing prompts, I told myself.

Except that other students *did* keep up with the prompts and turned in fat journals overflowing with the work they'd done. I couldn't deal with the idea that I'd been lazy or rebellious about the assignments. I simply decided it wasn't fair. And it was *her* fault for not making the assignments clearer.

She called me out. Told me to get it together and work it. Wondering how this beloved woman could treat me like this, I gradually pulled her down off the pedestal upon which I'd placed her.

I made an appointment to see her, to have a cup of coffee and talk to her about the class. In a tearful conversation, I told her that her directions as to homework and writing prompts were not clear. And none of it felt fair.

"How is it that other students understood the assignments and you didn't?" she asked.

In my most defensive voice, I said, "They've studied with you before." And as soon as I said it, I knew that it was lame, a blaming excuse. I could feel the heat rise in my cheeks as Susan reached out and took my hand in hers.

"There's a greater lesson here," she said. "You know I couldn't have lasted that much longer in the heights to which you elevated me."

I shook my head, still not ready to concede. I wanted to be the victim of overwhelm. "This is just too hard for me. It's too much," I whined.

Then she totally surprised me. While still holding my hand, she said, "Do the assignments. Turn them in, along with the new assignments, and you'll get through this class just fine. Otherwise, you're in danger of failing."

Just like that. *This cannot be happening*, I thought. Who fails a journal-writing class? So with a fair amount of anger and resentment, I wrote. I wrote my ass off and took square aim at the teacher who had disappointed me. I turned in the homework that I hadn't done, the assignments that I claimed were muddied due to her ineptness and the resulting confusion. When I got my journal back the following week, she handed it to me with a little smirk on her face.

"Good work," she said. "Glad to see you're in touch with your anger." And I had to grin. I had written pages and pages of anger and rage, and in the moment it didn't mean a whole lot, except that Susan's "write everything" motto for this class had somehow broken open in me all the places I could draw upon, both dark and light.

I never placed Susan on a pedestal again, but she remained forever my favorite teacher at Naropa. She helped me cut the thread of girlish confusion and then weave it into myself, completing the more mature woman I was becoming. Susan required that I finish the work at hand without complaint, ushering me to a place of emotional sobriety where I met my own competence.

When I think of her now, I remember the strong feminist that she was. There are some feminists that demonstrate a warrior-like strength when it comes to personal psychological work. They have a special understanding of what the word "forthright" means. Maybe it's that they've fought so hard to be seen as an equal. I wanted to be like Susan. In her work with me, she took away anyplace that I could have hidden or retreated to. She was in my face about the work of creativity, and how it was more perspiration than inspiration. I admired how strong and empowered she presented herself in the world. She was full in her authenticity, and she passed that lesson on to all of her students.

Susan came to my graduation, even though she no longer taught at Naropa. My heart swelled when I saw her sitting in the audience, knowing she was one of those women I'd never forget. She had always been in my court, even when she kicked my butt.

On graduation day, I took note of how she smiled and cheered for each of us as we walked across the stage to get our diploma. When it was time for me to collect mine, I had a sense I'd only made it that far because of her.

For a few years after I left Naropa, I continued to meet with Susan for lunch or coffee. And then marriage, a mortgage, and all the stuff of life got in the way of keeping up the relationship. I lost track of her for what seemed like just a short time. One day I heard that she'd died. I cried for her, cried because I hadn't seen her in a year or two. Cried because of course I should have known how fragile life is. Sometimes the people that make the biggest difference for us are the shortest relationships. She'd enlivened so much in me, all of it done with much love. She set me free, helping me to gain confidence and self-respect, to discover I didn't have to find another teacher to put on a pedestal; I only had to rise up to the occasion of being emotionally honest with myself.

The truth about older women, about women who fully embody the Creatrix, is that their wisdom nourishes and uplifts. Susan pushed me to accept I was strong, capable, and competent. The gift of self-reliance unfolded within me through her skillful midwifery, which wouldn't allow me to be any less than who I was truly meant to be. I didn't get my own self-worth at the time, so I saw it in her. Susan Edwards did what a good teacher does: she helped me get free from devaluing myself. I think of her often and wish that I could share with her all the adventures I've created, in part, because of her presence in my life. That's what good teachers do, and we never forget them as a result.

~~~~~~~~~

For Reflection, Activity, and Journaling

I was surprised when I journaled about a teacher I'd had in junior high school because I remembered so much about her and what our relationship was to one another. We all meet teachers throughout our school years, and sometimes it's the ones we meet later in life that have such a big impact. I bless the many teachers of my older years who have reminded me that psychological and spiritual growth does not have an end point. To live fully, you need to always be growing and changing.

1. Do you have a favorite teacher you remember from your school days? What is the lesson they imparted that you will never forget?

2. A woman embodying the qualities of the Creatrix can be teacher to a younger generation of women. How do you teach younger women in your life? What qualities do you bring to that teaching?

3. Is teaching a younger generation the imparting of a lesson, or is it something more, the modeling for how to live a full and loving life? Journal about how you are modeling, or may have modeled, that kind of life for a younger woman.

CHAPTER TWELVE

CREATRIX AS ILLUMINATOR

*E*normous in the sky, a full moon casts a glittering ribbon of light upon the dark, black waters, a path that if followed leads to the Weaver. Deep, deep down at the bottom of the ocean, the old woman, who does not remember how she came to be among the fishes and the coral, sits at a loom and weaves the loose weave of nets from seaweed strands brought to her by her dolphins. A shuttlecock made of shell moves back and forth, back and forth in her bony hand, stringing the weed over and under as the net takes shape. When finished, she will give it to you to cast into the realm of dreams, but you must know how to ask her for it—to tell her that you long to gather the inspirations and visions of what might come to be. You must ask her nicely and promise to pull those inspirations and visions revealed close to your heart. To nurture them with delicate care so they will grow.

I bring offerings to the Weaver of small, round stones and sea glass eroded by the undertow into smooth, shiny currency to lay at her feet. I wait for her to sing to me—long, beautiful, sad songs.

• • •

This was a dream I had when I was turning sixty. I didn't know it then, but the dream was an invitation. Not just an invitation to one thing, but an invitation to meet myself in new ways, to see myself in new ways, to gain my footing and confidence, or more aptly put, to do the work of my authentic heart.

My struggle in becoming a person who liked herself had a lot to do with the face I presented to the world and the face of who I felt I was on the inside. Often those faces did not match. It takes courage to be real. Living in a culture that emphasizes winning and losing, accumulation and accomplishment makes for a rough terrain on which to awaken authentically. The praise and accolades that come from outer successes are absent, as insights and revelations unfold within. The ongoing reinvention of self is a constant practice. Do the qualities of heart match the face that I present to the world? My sixties would be a time for me to realize my soul's dream of being awake and in love with life.

Becoming an older woman can be a time of psychological and spiritual grappling. It's like starting a new life. Who am I without my work to identify me? No longer young, how do I fit in? What is my value? And why at sixty am I still sorting out the pains of childhood?

Right around this edge of sixty, I met Reverend Cynthia James. Distance gives all of us better sight, and looking back, I realize that Cynthia held a light for me. She illuminated my path.

I met her through a phone call. I was working with my husband, running his front office. He was an integrative doctor in Boulder. One day, a man came to see him and took a seat in the waiting room. I saw that he was carrying a book—*What Will Set You Free*. Why did I want to see that man's book? I didn't usually ask people if I could look at what they were reading. His name has no place in my memory, but I bless him when I think back. He was a messenger. I met Cynthia James because this man was carrying her book.

"May I see your book?" I asked. He handed it to me. I scanned the table of contents and then read that the title had come from someone Cynthia had been working for at the time. He'd written a poem entitled "What Will Set You Free." He'd seen the phrase spray-painted on a freeway underpass in Los Angeles. At the same time, Cynthia was writing a book without a title, but when she heard her boss's poem, she asked if she could use the title.

I stopped reading, but held the book in my hand for another minute. I wanted to know too—what *will* set you free? I scribbled down Cynthia's name on a Post-it note and handed the book back to the man.

"Have you met her?" I asked.

"I go to Mile Hi," he said.

Mile Hi Church is affiliated with the United Centers for Spiritual Living, once known as the religious science movement. The church is located in Lakewood, Colorado, a sprawling Denver suburb. It sits in the middle of a large campus and is all about inclusion, love, and welcoming. Even though I'd known about the place for most of my years living in Boulder, it wasn't until I met Cynthia that I visited there. Cynthia James was an associate minister—an inspirational minister, to say the least. And she sang. The first time I heard her preach a sermon, she turned around and sang about it. How could one person possess so much talent, and how could I not be intrigued? Because of her, Mile Hi Church would become a home to me.

I didn't wait until I'd left the office. I got the number that I needed for the church, picked up the phone, and called

Cynthia. I'd been looking for someone to facilitate a retreat for my women's group, and I had this gut sense that I'd found her. Much to my surprise and delight, she was very easy to reach.

"A guy came into my office and showed me your book," I said to her. "I'd like to meet you and see if you'd be interested in conducting a one-day women's retreat." Just like that, no hesitation. No vetting. Just an instantaneous and impulsive trust that this was someone who was going to be part of my life. I remember that she laughed when I asked, a delighted laughter that fit our serendipitous encounter.

For the next few weeks, we talked regularly, hammering out the details of a women's retreat. When I finally met her in person, her image was nothing like what I'd expected. She wore her hair in what looked like hundreds of braids that hung halfway down her back. Her long skirts and loose jackets flowed when she walked, making her appear as if she floated into a room. I'd soon find out that all that gentleness, calm, and flowing didn't make her a pushover. She was by far the strongest woman I'd ever met. I was so in need of strength. Real woman strength, the kind that comes from the core of feeling good about who you are. The kind of strength born of self-respect.

Spending a day with her and the women in my group was a satisfying retreat experience. In fact, it was probably the last high point of the women's group I'd started. Cynthia had an unwavering commitment to help women live their potential.

The question that dogged me after our time together that day was, What else? I wanted to know more about her work and what she did. How did she know that working with women was her calling? How was she growing older so gracefully and with such power? How did she get to be so self-assured? Of course, those questions weren't really directed at her—they were questions for me. They were part of my own grappling.

Soon after the retreat, I signed up to take the Beyond Limits class that she taught at Mile Hi. In a classroom of thirty men and women, we met a few times a week. I brought a spiral notebook to take notes, and while I'm sure she was a good teacher, what she gave me was less about the lesson plan and more about how she comported herself in the classroom.

I felt intimidated at times, not by her but by my own lack of confidence. As an exercise for myself, each time I stood in her classroom to ask a question or share an observation, I said these words out loud: "I stand in the light of my truth," and then I'd get on with what I had to say or ask. It was a scary ritual, one that took some courage. No one had told me to say it; I made it up for myself as a challenge. At that time, in that class, those words meant a great deal to me—I wanted to know my own light, and I was thinking about and turning over in my mind just what my truth was. What does it mean to stand in the light of one's truth? It was the question I held in my heart. This is why that statement was the perfect thing for me to say each time I spoke, because doing so made me continue the great grappling, the examination of what it was I believed, and what it meant to be true to myself.

One day a man in our classroom stood up and started to talk about a project he was conducting. Cynthia stopped him.

"I appreciate your commitment to your project," she said, "but this is not a place for promoting." The man continued anyway.

"I'm asking you to stop," she said. He pushed back, continuing with a website address for the project.

"Stop," Cynthia said to him, staring him down. "This is my classroom, and as such, you will abide by my rules, or you will leave."

My heart was racing. I was uncomfortable with confrontation. I squirmed in my seat. I grew warm and sweaty. At the same time, I was fascinated by how Cynthia was so at ease, so much in command—not in a bitchy or mean way, but in a forthright way that set boundaries. (Damn, why do I always think *bitch* or *bitchy* when women are just standing up for themselves?) I wasn't good at the boundary thing. I always thought about what I could have said or should have said long after the fact.

When the interaction was over, the promoter sat down, and Cynthia picked up the lesson plan, continuing.

I raised my hand. "Wait," I said. "How did you do that? I'm sitting here shaking about a confrontation that isn't even mine. If it were mine, I don't think I would have been able to be so direct. How did you do that?" I felt like a little kid asking the big kid how to ride a bike.

"Practice," she said. "Practice setting boundaries for yourself as an act of self-love. Know that confidence, believing in yourself, and strength are the result of practice."

Maybe those weren't her exact words, but they do express the exact message I hold in memory. *Practice.* Life is a practice. Becoming a mature woman is practice. I learn one thing and then move on to the next thing, and I've never gotten all of it right. No one ever does. I was then, and continue to be, a woman who is sad and happy, confident and afraid, self-doubting as well as self-confident. The difference between then and now, though, is that I don't judge myself for any of those things. Every emotion, every experience becomes part of who I am. Cynthia James held a light to that fact.

For two years in a row, Cynthia facilitated the retreat for my women's group. Then, when my women's group broke apart, breaking my heart with it, I turned to her with the tatters of my failure. I had difficulty in coming to terms with how much I was responsible for what happened to my group and how some of it was just a stupid power play that had gotten out of control between one of the other women and myself. When everything came crashing down, Cynthia welcomed me with arms of comfort.

I followed her around for a couple of years, the little sister wanting to be like the big sister. It was two years of an ongoing conversation. All of what I imagined to be broken in me I laid bare in weekly sessions of spiritual guidance until I touched the deep sorrow I'd been dealing with.

I was diagnosed with depression in my early thirties and medicated soon thereafter. Funny thing, initially I was relieved that the sorrow had a name and hopeful the medication would take the edge off. But I only took the medication for a few days. The drugs made me feel like a zombie, and it didn't make sense that I'd worked so hard to clean up my life from recreational drugs and now I was taking "sanctioned" drugs. Something in me knew this was not the route I wanted to go. I stopped seeing the psychiatrist that had medicated me and spent the next thirty years coming to terms with the difference between depression and sorrow.

There is no diagnostic code for grief, and there are no medications for sorrow. There is therapy, some of it helpful and some of it not. There are workshops and places where you can explore your sadness. But as a rule, the up-and-down ride of feeling broken and then fixed is just that: a ride, and not a destination. I've met healers who claim to have some special power that will take away what ails you. But where I've found the most comfort has been in the gentle kind of reflection and contemplation that leads to a rigorous honesty. Then comes the work of gratitude after the dust has settled, and that's what makes me feel whole. I'd rather cry than be a zombie. How many women get that choice? Women in this country remain the most overmedicated group when it comes to depression treatment.

I gave myself to weekly sessions of spiritual guidance with Cynthia. I took her workshop that she ran every year at Mile Hi called What Will Set You Free, named after her book. I followed her to retreats and lectures, and this is what she gave to me: I gained the courage to face myself just as I am, without apology. It didn't heal me, but it gave me the strength of options—how to do or see things differently. It made me want to practice self-love.

I still sometimes meet the demons of "not good enough" and "I don't belong." Through facing the worst fears and judgments about myself, a tender acceptance and self-empathy has taken root. I've been able to manage the sorrow and the grief. I've learned to open myself to grace and to understand that compassion is not just being nice to someone else. It's knowing the pain in my heart that allows me to empathize with others.

When I met Cynthia, I was embarrassed by my personal pain. Other people seemed to be doing life so differently, so much better than I was. The word I think best describes who Cynthia was to me is *illuminator*. She shined light and allowed spaciousness for every emotion of my heart to have air. Hanging on so tightly to sadness so no one else will see is what keeps it around. Once my feelings had permission, a kind of validation, I no longer felt stuck. The experience of sharing my grief with someone else is what helped loosen its grip, and I could let it go.

At times in my life, women like Cynthia appeared unapproachable, as if they possessed a magical knowledge that I could never reach. I was on the outside looking in. But that feeling was soon to be dissipated. Toward the end of the two years I followed her around, Cynthia shared with me that she taught a class at the Jefferson County Detention Center. I can't quite recall how I followed in her footsteps. Did I ask her for a contact there? Did she offer it? Even though the details are sketchy, what stays with me are the results. I became a volunteer at the Jefferson County Detention Center, and for three years, I taught creative writing to incarcerated women at that facility.

Teaching a group of women who were struggling with many of the same issues I'd struggled with, or was currently struggling with, made me see the world differently. I was blessed. I was privileged. And most of all I was honored to be with women in their struggle and offer them ideas and a creative outlet. When I taught my classes, I brought a little iPod dock and played beautiful classical music. I turned them on to Chopin's piano concertos, to Yo-Yo Ma playing the unaccompanied Cello Suites. We used music as a backdrop for writing, for relaxing. It was a special moment in their week to be enveloped in beauty when so much of their lives had not been beautiful at all.

I loved all those women as if they were my daughters. In many ways they were. I could have easily wound up at someplace like the Jefferson County Detention Center myself. It was only dumb luck and not getting caught that prevented it. And I created some resources that allowed me to climb out of the world of smart-ass, streetwise kids and into a world of kind and wiser women. Loving those women at the detention center was an extension of learning to love myself. The analogy of prison and self-imprisonment was not lost on me.

To become a wise elder is to answer the calling to fulfill one's purpose. At the threshold of old age, there are two directions that can be taken. One path points to the lamentation of lost youth, an unwinnable battle with wrinkles, the loss of athletic prowess, and graying hair. Taking this direction will be met with chants of regret for things that will never return. The voice of railing against growing older and becoming more mature is a bitter one that clouds the eyes and contracts the heart.

The other path is the path of purpose, which requires courage, conviction, and a new vision for the future. Take this path and you begin to grow downward as well as upward. I love the image of the old oak tree as a symbol for the third chapter of life. The branches reach upward into the heavens, and the roots stretch downward into the dark, reaching for the waters of compassion.

The misconception of the wise elder is that she's someone who tells you how to be wise. That's just a stereotype. The wise elder has surrendered to and is empowered by an integrity of love, and like the old woman at the bottom of the sea in my dream, she weaves a net that she will give to the younger women. The wise elder demonstrates a life that inspires.

And how does she do that? By living in an integrity that shines a light of love into the world. This is what it means to be generous of spirit. And that's who Cynthia was to me, a woman of generous spirit, a mentor, and an illuminator. It wasn't that she had wise words for me, though there were wise words spoken. It was the way she walked through life. She lived out of a constant love and had mastered the art of deep listening. These pointed to the qualities of being a true elder.

Cynthia never really taught me anything, and she taught me everything. She didn't hold any magic answers to the pain in my life. But she modeled for me how a strong woman gathers sustenance from her core and brings it forward.

Because of her, I came to find beauty and gratitude within myself that blooms in day-to-day living. I grew psychologically and spiritually, and continue to experience grace because of those blessed individuals, like Cynthia, who are in my orbit. Nothing I have accomplished or realized has been possible without the women around me. That's a life truth and my greatest motivation for wanting to be an uplifter for others, because I have been lifted up and held up so many times, by so many women.

As we grow into the Creatrix, we reach back to bring others with us. To be an older woman is a noble thing. Becoming an older woman holds the potential to witness one's calling and purpose come to fruition. I am blessed to have known so many women, to have had friendships in which I bear witness to the process of aging and also to the process of realization that we are more deeply beautiful than ever before.

I stand in the light of my truth. . . .

~~~~~~~~~~

For Reflection, Activity, and Journaling

The Creatrix was passed a torch by the women who came before her, the women who paved a way and paid a price. Now we hold a light, and that light we hold guides us both outwardly and into the inner life. To live an empowered life, we grow upward, and we grow downward, too, a mirror of the tree, rooted in heaven as well as in the earth.

1. What is your path of conviction and purpose in this world? What do you stand for?

2. Who has held a light for you in your life? What were the circumstances of being led out of the dark?

3. Who have you held a light for? A friend? A family member? Journal about that relationship. How did you help that person? Did you feel confident in helping through encouragement, deep listening, being nonjudgmental, and creating a safe space for the other person to vent?

PART FOUR:

CELEBRATING THE CREATRIX

In our evolution as women, we have graduated from the insult of Crone to the celebration of the Creatrix. The arc of that education extends from an outdated myth that a woman beyond her mothering years is used up, insignificant, and irrelevant—the Crone—to a higher ground where a new archetype exists: the Creatrix. Within this new archetype, the midlife woman weaves the qualities of intuition, imagination, and creativity, cultivated in her maturity, into the whole cloth of a life. The woof and warp that form the foundation of this new archetype stand out in brilliant threads of strength, resiliency, and courage.

Midlife women and women beyond midlife no longer accept the story once written for them by men. They are no longer intimidated or limited by it. We are moving into a new story, as we stand at the precipice of being emboldened on our journey. It's time now to throw a stake into the ground and claim the power of being a mature woman.

As the saying goes, "Those who do not remember the past are doomed to repeat it." We cannot throw out or disregard our history. Therefore, we cannot just get rid of the Crone. We have to take a good, long look at her, and see her for the shadow part of ourselves that she is. For a long time, the Crone dominated our self-image, and so she deserves to be thanked and honored as part of our feminist history. The Crone was once seen as a signpost that devalued a woman's midlife passage rather than celebrating it. The Crone had little power in the past, but the Creatrix gently reassigns the Crone's place in our lineage to the dark and shadowy place where she warns of the trap of not believing in yourself. She holds the cautionary tale of how that happens when we let others define us. In this way, we are able to learn from her and listen to her.

There's no doubt that older women have reached a tipping point in their evolution. The cumulative effect of so many little steps has resulted in one big step, after which nothing will ever look the same. We need to remind ourselves that as with all kinds of evolution, there is no destination point, no complete, all-the-way healing, but rather more unfolding, more work to be done. We grow psychologically and spiritually until the time we die.

The nature of who we have become and who we are becoming is revealed in how we are reimagining our personal lives as well as the world around us. The Creatrix nature shows itself in deepening conversations and a desire to uplift other women. It redefines what being beautiful is. And it asks us to relegate the Crone to her rightful place, as a keeper of cautionary tales and testimony. May the Crone remind us of the distance women have traveled to gain a still-growing equality. While that equality may not always be seen in the world, the Creatrix sees it in herself, and she will not give up the good fight.

CHAPTER THIRTEEN

CELEBRATE FRIENDSHIPS

As a little girl, I knew the way I lived was different from the way other kids lived. My family was made up of only my mom and me. We lived in duplexes and apartment buildings that were on the boulevard. Our home hummed with the sound from busy streets while the homes behind us stretched into quiet neighborhoods with traditional families. Other moms didn't work. They, instead, organized bake sales and mother-daughter fashion shows at the elementary school. In this 1960s version of reality, happiness eluded me.

When I was in the sixth grade, I decided I didn't want to be different. What I wanted more than anything was to fit in. What I didn't know yet was that fitting in is not the same as belonging, that the price of curated friends who make you feel like you fit in means giving up certain truths about yourself. I developed a narrative while in the sixth grade in which I started to lie about who my father was, what he did. I told people he was the editor of a big newspaper on the East Coast. I said that he was very, very rich. I carried around a picture of my dad and me standing in front of a large apartment building and showed it to classmates, telling them that it wasn't an apartment building at all; it was the mansion my dad lived in.

My lies were easy to keep up or change because my mom moved us each year, and that meant a new school and a whole new group of kids, so I never really had to come clean to anyone. I think I probably lied about my background and my dad because I felt lonely, and I thought if I were richer or better or cooler, I would fit in. Big chunks of time went by, years when I didn't see my siblings, let alone my dad. From the age of twelve until I was twenty-five, I didn't see him even once. A decade or more passed without seeing my brother or sister. These big gaps without any family resulted in a nervous energy of self-disdain and longing to fit in that followed me around every day. And then I met Kitty.

A Polaroid from the summer of 1973 shows the two of us huddled over slices of birthday cake. We're standing in the reception area of *Penthouse* magazine, where Kitty is an assistant editor. We are in the foreground; a blurred background of models on the arms of much older men is behind us. This is my friend Kitty's twenty-first birthday. The photograph shows two barely legal women not even trying to look glamorous or sophisticated. Instead two girls are hunched over a paper plate of birthday cake, looking like gleeful ten-year-olds.

We'd come back from the fire escape, having smoked a joint and made catty remarks about all the models who'd stopped by for cake and champagne. It helped us feel less awkward, feel better about ourselves. Then we inhaled birthday cake and ignored the backdrop of leggy models and older men.

It was shortly after that party, celebrating twenty-one, that we became roommates. We had a house in Laurel Canyon that leaked like crazy in the winter rains. But it made up for its leaks and drips with a living room that had a fireplace and

French windows that opened onto sky. Laurel Canyon was all hills and streets that climbed from the canyon floor, and it always felt to me like we lived in the clouds.

We furnished the house with donations and garage sales, and a little help from Kitty's mother, and then got down to the business of living. Out on our own, young in the world, Kitty worked at *Penthouse*, and I landed work at a television show called *The Midnight Special*. That show turned out to be a precursor for MTV and a long line of music videos, more proof that Alan Freed, the 1950s disc jockey, had been right in his prediction—rock 'n' roll was here to stay.

Life couldn't be any cooler. Musicians stopped by our house and played new songs they'd written. A country music star I knew fell onto Kitty's bed one night and passed out. We woke him up with water and laughter, showing him to my room, where he passed out again. An artist who lived down the hill brought flowers and drawings of flowers that he left under our doormat. A constant stream of runners from television shows and low-level production assistants like me came and went with baggies of pot and the willingness to share. The music of Joni Mitchell and Linda Ronstadt filled the air, a soundtrack to a life I wanted to last forever. For a moment, it seemed like it would, until life, as it always does, intervened.

We can't fully grow up without love or a feeling of belonging. Kitty was my belonging. I didn't think so much about fitting in with her. I was already home. Sometimes she was like a sister, and sometimes she was like a mother. More than friendship, she passed on life essentials that no one else had taught me. How to open a savings account. Pay the rent on time. Don't stay up all night partying and blow off work the next day. And my favorite bit of twenty-one-year-old wisdom: no guys can spend the night here unless you've dated them for ninety days. Kitty's philosophy was that anyone can keep up party manners for ninety days, and then they start to show you who they are. I never waited ninety days on anything carnal, but I liked the philosophy anyway.

Before Kitty, there'd been no longtime best friend in my life. Although I'd made friends, a lifetime of moving from apartment to apartment and always changing schools had prevented me from finding peers whose presence could bring me comfort and a sense of place in the world. As a result, I was destined to carry a lifetime of thinking I was on the outside looking in. For that one brief time in the early 1970s, in Laurel Canyon when the Joni Mitchell album *Ladies of the Canyon* filled the rooms of our house and wafted from the windows onto the streets, I belonged to youth and all its coolness. I belonged to my friend Kitty.

Kitty came from a real family with a mom, a dad, and a brother. Both she and her brother were adopted, and early on she shared with me her longing to find her birth family. It was a quest for her. She wanted to know where she came from and how she belonged. Listening to her talk about belonging was like a permission slip for me. I stopped lying about my family and began the long road to self-acceptance and self-love. I was not alone anymore. Kitty was my first true friend. I didn't have to impress her or be a certain way in order to be with her. I began to see that friendship was more about belonging.

In the journey of becoming the person that I am, I've made women friends all over this country. I feel like I'm part of a sisterhood of women, that I'm never really alone, that I belong. I'm a nomad. I can't remember all of the addresses where I've lived. Yet there's a familiarity in my bones in moving from one place to another. A sense of new beginning, of reinvention, of awakening. Like the little girl in the duplex on the boulevard, my life is different from the way a lot of people live. But I no longer feel I have to fit in or that I'll be rejected because I'm different.

Kitty and I are still friends, and in spite of several interstate moves on my part, we've stayed in touch, and our heart connection has never wavered. Because of her, I was able to make lots of women friends in my life, and I've gotten better at being a good friend as I've gotten older.

Every woman has a story about connecting with other women. For some, it's been easy. For others it's been difficult, and for most of us it's been a combination of the two. In spite of our deep longings, sometimes we just don't connect or know where or how to begin. I think I've been a really good friend sometimes, and I feel like this is an area that will always be a work in progress for me.

I met a young woman a few years ago who was a schoolteacher. She was writing a book for her middle-grade students. The book was titled *I See You and You Matter*. I don't know if she ever got it published, and I don't remember the story she was trying to tell, but the title of that book stayed with me because this is what we are all seeking: to be seen. To matter.

I doubt that any of us really grow psychologically or spiritually without the help of other women. Friendships are more than companionship, more than fitting in. Women friends help our confidence to grow, and we become more adroit at listening to one another. As more of us feel seen and feel that we matter, we become more emotionally available in our relationships, and therefore bring about the kinds of conversations that can create change. It's in women's nature to want to make the deep dive, to mine the heart for our greatest potential. We are, at midlife, witnessing each other as we learn to embody the emerging midlife archetype of the Creatrix and extend friendship to others who are in the process of becoming that, too.

For Reflection, Activity, and Journaling

We crave closeness and connection, and too often we try to let our texts, emails, and Zoom calls fill that longing. In the mask-wearing time of Coronavirus, when it's difficult to interact with people, seeing only half of a face adds yet another dimension of unreachability. But even before the virus, we were headed down that road, too enamored with our devices.

Something we can do now is make sure that our conversations are real, that we value emotional honesty, and that we don't feel it necessary to fill up every single space with our words. The most meaningful conversations are ones where we listen intently before we start thinking about how we want to respond.

1. Think about the conversations you are having with other women. How might you use listening/witnessing as a way to bring about growth and transformation?

2. How do you let people know that they matter to you?

3. Questions are a good way to show the other person you're listening. That you can ask a question based on something they've just told you shows that you're interested in them. Try this: Before you meet with a friend, set an intention in your own heart and mind to be a source of positivity and encouragement. Be someone who listens.

CHAPTER FOURTEEN

CELEBRATE SOUL WORK

Let the beauty we love be what we do.
There are hundreds of ways to kneel and kiss the ground.

When I read that line from the seventeenth-century poet Rumi's book, *The Book of Love: Poems of Ecstasy and Longing*, I think of *soul work*. Soul work is what we are called to do as we get older. It's an investigation and redefinition of what it means to be beautiful and how that beauty is a doorway to creativity and gratitude.

Growing older, I don't want to lament the loss of physical beauty, even though sometimes I'm not thrilled with what is sagging. When author Nora Ephron titled a book she wrote later in life *I Feel Bad About My Neck*, I understood that frame of mind completely. As I'm letting go of a now-withered youthful beauty, I aspire to pay homage to the beauty of my soul, so alive and vibrant in these later years. Learning to love one's self is not only the purview of young women but a lifelong practice of self-acceptance at every age, especially acute as the body goes through the changes of breakdown and inevitable obsolescence.

I've often joked that my skin losing its elasticity is God's way of pulling me to my knees. Humility is the friend of maturation. There's a lot of empathy and compassion that gets born by the grace of growing older and its accompanying humility. I find myself frequently reevaluating what's really important. For me, it's that I want to be a light in the world. I want to share the hard-won wisdom that comes with maturity, and I don't need a face-lift to do that.

The inner work of midlife women is to make peace with all of the physical and emotional changes of growing older, finding celebration and joy in the passage as we gather strength, courage, and the voice of wisdom with which to leave the world a better place.

And yes, it's a climb, a rocky one at that, but it's the work of finding soul beauty, the power, love, and rapture of a life that we've served and has served us. Midpoint in a woman's life, when children are grown and careers have been fed, is a time of new opening and new vision.

For me that happened while I was in my midfifties. I visited a friend who had a small dog. One day, the dog jumped up into my lap. I love animals. Love dogs. So, I let the little creature make herself comfortable while I cooed and stroked her head. My friend, sitting across a wide expanse of desk from where I sat, picked up her camera and began clicking away. Head still bent, my eyes found the camera lens, and I smiled. Shutter. Click. Shutter. Click. And then the dog jumped out of my lap and made her way back to whatever small dogs do during the day while my friend and I continued our conversation.

Fast-forward a couple of weeks—the friend emailed me the photos. "Thought you'd like these. Look how adorable you guys are!" her email read.

I opened the attachment, excited to see the little dog and not expecting to see the old woman. When did I get three or four double chins when my head bent forward? When had my skin wrinkled and my smile drooped at the corners? I didn't like the way I looked. It was a shock. How had my face changed so much?

Once, when I was twenty-two, I surprised myself when catching my reflection in a mirror. I remember lingering for a moment. The person looking back at me was a young woman, no longer a girl, a beauty born of youth. And now, thirty-five years later, the reflection I'd seen then had changed to reflect someone else.

There is a period of grief when we know for sure that youth has left us. A moment like the one with the dog in my lap, captured in a photograph that looks nothing like the way I felt on the inside. The word *resignation* hangs unwelcoming in the air.

I'm not against face-lifts, but even with one, eventually we are rendered mature. I believe it is part of a spiritual unfolding to love our older years. Without letting go of the trappings of youth and its reflection, one will never be able to sit quietly and contemplate the gentle embrace of the spirit. Soul work—the work of the authentic heart—is the wisdom work that comes with embodying the Creatrix.

My hands have maps of veins and tendons, marking everything I ever grasped or released. One leg shows a bulging vein that begins midshin and crawls up to the side of my knee. I often wonder about painting it with henna and turning it into a gnarled tree trunk with leaves and toadstools. A whimsical piece of art made from my aging legs that still grace me with the strength of long walks and afternoon swims.

We leave one beauty behind us for another that rises with the moon. Youthful beauty is gone for good, along with late-night dancing and early spring mornings wrapped up in quilts with a lover. Now, we sit among other silver-haired women, holding on to chipped cups, reading meaning into the last bit of afternoon tea. Somehow, to each other we all seem so lovely, but it's not a physical beauty anymore. It's something beyond the quiet and appreciative conversations. How can we not marvel at the dreams and magic held in our hearts, eternal and unlimited? We all hope to die with dreams in our hearts and the poetry of magic on our lips. This is what I tell myself, anyway. I tell myself there is great power in the sharing of stories.

I listen for tales of what used to be then, and what will be now. Husbands lost. A child sometimes. Siblings. I listen to the pain and the passion bend and blend into one thing, and am reminded of Rumi's words: "Let the beauty we love be what we do."

The rising voices of the Creatrix gain traction as they are pulled toward the crown of the wise woman. The Creatrix begins the work of deepening her inner journey at midlife. She learns to trust the receding of youthful beauty and the replacement of soul beauty. Her heart swells as she connects to the reverence of maturation, a creative unfolding that will be the tail of her bright star as it streaks across the sky.

This poem came upon me one morning as I was having my tea on the back porch, and I quickly grabbed a pen and paper to capture its words:

Made from stardust,
the ancient Godhead hums
a lullaby's lament
for all the broken hearts

Swaddled in the night sky,
an unmoving Grace
the meadow's mist
ghostly outlines fence posts

Lying down in her light,
soothed by the song
the rising lingers
on eternity's horizon

As the soul drinks
moonlight nectar
origins remembered
in love's illumination

To watch the beauty of one's younger life transform to the deepening beauty of one's soul is to surrender to the miracle of creation, the cycle of the seasons, and the abiding rapture of being alive.

For Reflection, Activity, and Journaling

Work defines us. Relationships define us. Family defines us. As a result, it can sometimes feel like we are absent from knowing ourselves as we get older. Soul work is the personal work of reflecting on your psychological and spiritual life and making choices about how to nurture yourself inwardly.

In music, it's not just the notes you play; it's the spaces between the notes, the notes you don't play, that lend themselves to the character of a piece of music. In life, it's not all the ways you fill up the time; it's the space where there is no one but you. That's the place where you can ask yourself, Am I at peace with myself? Am I happy? Am I growing into a better person? What can I do to nurture the values I hold dear, like kindness, compassion, beauty, and joy?

In that vein, here are some questions to reflect upon:

1. Can you rest in the new beauty that is older age? In what ways can you cultivate and nourish the beauty of your heart? What can you tell yourself about the goodness of your heart?

2. How would you describe yourself, using only positive words? Write them down. Breathe deeply and let yourself take in the description.

3. Where have you seen the most growth and change in your life in the past year?

4. Do you have a practice that allows you the pleasure of just hanging out with yourself and enjoying your own

company? Yoga and meditation come to mind, but you can also try things like coloring, doodling, or working with clay. Quiet activities that bring out your creative nature can be a good way to contemplate the current state of your life. It's not about judging yourself; it's about asking yourself what's next for your psychological and spiritual growth.

CHAPTER FIFTEEN

CELEBRATE FORGIVENESS

AND GRACE

We cannot grow into the potential and possibility of the Creatrix archetype unless we are intimately familiar with forgiveness. Experience has taught me that forgiveness is not a one-time deal. There's a biblical reference to forgiveness that says we must forgive "not seven times, but seventy-seven times" (Matt. 18:21). Those wise words illustrate that forgiveness is not some sort of benediction or affirmation. Rather, forgiveness is a process that takes both time and practice, thus the reference to "seventy-seven times."

Forgiveness begins with forgiving yourself. Once you forgive yourself, you're able to more easily forgive others. This is a story about forgiving myself and learning that the result of self-forgiveness is grace.

◆ ◆ ◆

I was an embarrassed thirty-five-year-old. I was working in a law office in the afternoons and going to school in the mornings. It wasn't easy going back to pick up the pieces of a life I'd rejected fifteen years ago. At a time when most of my peers were beginning to enjoy the success of their families and careers, shame and the right amount of hope became the motivators for going back to school.

I never finished high school. When I'd first dropped out, it seemed like a cool thing to do. I thought I would go to Los Angeles and write songs. I thought I'd fall in love. I thought I'd be so relieved to be away from home. All of that proved to be wrong fairly quickly. I had some great moments in Los Angeles, false starts that might have grown into something good, but I was a champion at sabotaging opportunity. A single choice, like dropping out of school, fed a festering self-disdain, and it wasn't until my third decade when I was more than halfway to forty that I decided going back to school was an option for me.

I'd stopped doing any drugs, even pot, and I was attending a Unity Church in Santa Monica, which gave me a place to check in with something good one time a week. That may sound like a really small thing, but because of my weekly attendance, a little spark of self-love started to grow in me. I don't think I even knew it at the time.

One Sunday, the minister asked us to write down a question and said he would try to answer as many as he could. Paper and pencils were passed out, and I wrote down my question, folded the small piece of paper, and put it into the basket being passed down the aisle. *How do you know when you're doing God's will?* Mine was the first question he pulled out of the basket.

"You know you're doing God's will," the minister said, "when you are in touch with the deepest feelings of your heart, and you begin to act upon those."

I'd hurt myself by dropping out of school. The pain of that regret loomed large in my life, a constant drone of anger at myself and the feeling of being a screwup. So I took the minister's words to heart, and I ran with them. Within a week, I had enrolled at Santa Monica College, ready to begin the spring semester. That decision would be one of the deepest and most profound healings in my life. It was the exact place and time where I began to forgive myself.

In my first year at the college, a fellow student introduced me to an older guy named Smokey. I fell into the habit of having coffee with Smokey every morning, just before I tortured myself in the math lab. In the short time I knew him, he became a friend, a father figure, a mentor, and a larger-than-life inspiration. I don't remember, or maybe I never asked, how he got a name like Smokey, but it suited him. His hair was the color of soft gray smoke. He was seventy-five years old and completing his last year at the college, majoring in comparative French literature. He'd go on to UCLA the next year and graduate with a bachelor of arts two years after that.

My relationship with Smokey was as if I'd started a conversation with him one day, and the conversation turned into a story. At first, the story was all about how he became a college student in his seventies. And knowing what he'd gone through to get here began to color the way I held my own story. Being with Smokey, I started to feel courageous, instead of feeling like a screwup.

None of us have memories that retain the exact facts. Memory is a mix of emotion and physical sensation. The gaps are filled in by imagination. We all see life through a slightly different lens, and that colors memory, too. So I can't recall the exact words Smokey said to me about being a young man in 1941, only that when he'd graduated from high school, he enrolled in college. But in December of that year, Pearl Harbor was bombed, and Smokey knew he wanted to fight for his country. Higher education got put on the back burner.

He showed me a picture of himself once. It was a formal black-and-white portrait in a simple wooden frame. He was wearing an army uniform and looking directly into the camera, his face solemn to match the soberness of the time. Did I see that his eyes were filled with ideals and dreams about who he hoped to become in the world? Was there fear in those eyes? He said he felt the world had come off its tracks and he wanted to help fix it. I didn't know how to tell him that my world had come off the tracks, too, and I was wanting to fix it. Somehow, next to his story, mine seemed shallow. So many of the obstacles in my life had been self-imposed.

Smokey came back from World War II with all his limbs and faculties intact. He hoped to pick up his college education where he'd left off. He married his high school sweetheart, and she got pregnant right away. Again, college was put on the back burner. It was hard not to feel a little guilty hearing about what Smokey had sacrificed compared to what I'd thrown away. With a wife and child, he found what he called "a really good job." A welder was happy to give him an apprenticeship. That led to Smokey going into the wrought iron business.

The feeling I had then and the feeling I have now is one of deep admiration for a seventy-year-old man who fought in a war, raised a family, made sure his sons got to go to college, and created a successful career in the wrought iron business. He eventually bought the company. He lived a lifetime before he retired. With kids grown and taken care of, grandchildren, and his sweetheart still at his side, Smokey was finally able to go to college. I've always loved stories about second chances and reinvention.

His story humbled me, inspired me, and filled me with the courage of possibility. For me, putting off school in my younger days had to do with youthful acting out and a ton of familial dysfunction. The path that brought me to college was not nearly as noble as Smokey's had been. Hearing his story gave me great comfort, though. If he could get through school at his age, I could certainly get through school at mine.

One afternoon, just before he was about to graduate from community college and move on to finish a degree at UCLA, Smokey invited a few of us over to his house. He lived in a modest neighborhood near the college in the same house where he'd raised his kids. We sat at a garden table on the front patio. I had to smile when I saw the railings around the porch and on the stairs. They were, of course, crafted of a beautiful wrought iron. His wife, a kind woman, welcomed her husband's young friends as if we were incredibly special. That's what good people do. They make you feel special. It was a trait I hoped to learn. She brought out a plate of cookies and a pitcher of lemonade before she disappeared back into the house. We sat around the patio table, talking about our futures. Smokey wanted to get his degree in comparative literature.

By my second year at Santa Monica College, Smokey had left and moved on to UCLA. His brief presence in my life made me stand a little bit straighter and walk with a little more purpose in my step. Smokey kindled in me a desire to forgive myself, and I began to realize how much not forgiving myself had held me back.

Midlife is a time that we get our ducks in a row. We choose to answer or ignore a calling. We find purpose or unrelenting grief. We either learn a self-love that gives us peace and courage, or we are unable to move forward. Without forgiveness, there is only being stuck.

Smokey showed me something else, too, that I draw upon today, some thirty-five years later: he showed me how a person stays engaged in life and continues to keep dreams alive, regardless of age or a thought to running out of time.

I still think of him. I doubt he's still in this world, but I know he'll always be alive in my heart. Smokey hoped to go to France after he graduated, to show his wife places he'd been during the war. I think he wanted to go back to Paris, a city he'd fallen in love with as a young soldier. He'd go back with a command of the language and relive the beauty and the feeling of the place, even though that place had been discovered under the worst of times.

I understand wanting to return to the place where you've fought. I understand wanting to let go of ancient sufferings and replace them with loveliness. That's what self-forgiveness does. It opens the door to grace. We cannot fully step into our power unless we can forgive ourselves for all sins, real and imagined. It's not that we have to forget. Choices, even bad ones, teach us things about ourselves. Self-forgiveness gives us a path to move forward. Self-forgiveness opens the door to living life on our own terms.

Just as Smokey would return to Paris to see the place with fresh eyes, I was able to return to myself with fresh eyes. I was not a horrible, terrible screwup of a person. I was a flawed person with a good heart, and that self-acknowledgment continues to carry me on the wings of striving for good and seeing good in others.

For Reflection, Activity, and Journaling

There have been times when forgiving myself felt out of reach, or when forgiving someone else did not seem possible. I know that forgiveness can happen in an instant because you decide to do it, and I also know that forgiveness often takes the path of a process, that it doesn't happen in one bite. Sometimes it takes coming back again and again to a grievance before you can let it go, forgive, and move on. That's what letting go means: moving on, not staying stuck in what is unfair or upsetting.

How do you get to that deeper part of yourself that reveals your intent and sincerity toward forgiveness of others and forgiveness of self? Contemplate that question as you respond to the following:

1. Explore the physical sensations of forgiveness: a softening in the heart area, a dropping of your shoulders. Your breathing may change. Lie on your back with your eyes closed, and breathe in a sense of release. Forgiveness can be one small step at a time in this way, a beginning of your "seventy-seven."

2. I find that gratitude helps me when I need to forgive myself or others. Sit in a comfortable position or lie down, with no distractions. Breathe in *thank you* and breathe out *thank you*. The thank-you doesn't even need to be attached to anything.

3. What are some other ways you can create softness and release, even if for a short time, that take your attention off a grievance about yourself or another?

Chapter Sixteen

Celebrate Your Story

We had come for a weekend visit, my mother and I. We'd sleep in Grandmother Julia's guest room, under the featherbed quilt that reminded me of snowy hills. Above us was a trapdoor that led to the attic. My mother pulled me close.

"Do you know what's up there?" she asked.

"Christmas decorations?"

"No. Dolls live in the attic, and after midnight they come alive."

"What kind of dolls?"

"Little Women dolls, like the two you have at home," my mother said, referring to the dolls made by Madame Alexander and inspired by the Louisa May Alcott novel.

While sleep pushed against my eyes, my mother told me the story of the dolls and how they had tea parties every night, about how when it snowed, they took little sleds up to the roof and rode them down to the gutters, laughing all the way. She told me about how the dolls made their own clothes

129

from scraps of material they found on my grandmother's sewing table. They made their own furniture from wooden spools my grandmother saved in her drawer.

Just before I surrendered to sleep, I turned my head and saw Julia standing in the doorway. She was smiling. I must have smiled back before I drifted off to sleep. The dolls visited me in nighttime visions, these small characters who transported me to an idea that I wanted to live life on my own terms as they did. I wanted to ride sleds in the winter snow. I wanted to come alive after midnight and have tea parties. I dreamed to the ticking of the oversized clock and awoke to the meadowlarks' song. I stared at the trapdoor in the ceiling before getting out of bed and wondered if the dolls had gone back to sleep.

The story of the dolls in the attic was one of the first stories I can remember my mother telling me. Stories were something that were made up, that could take me to places in my imagination where I could see other worlds and possibilities. The telling of the tale ignited in me a love of stories, books, and films. Later in life, I read books by May Sarton and Anaïs Nin, and realized my own life was a story, too.

Every woman I've ever met has a rich collection of stories within her. We weave together tales of our past and present, helping us make sense of the ideal we strive for: the freedom to do life on our own terms. The value in knowing the feminist history within our families helps us see ourselves more clearly, and the value of our personal history and progression hopefully inspires us to continue working toward equality of the sexes. Knowing our personal story without apology or shame opens the door to self-knowledge, and self-knowledge is a powerful thing. From the roots of self-knowledge, we mature and grow into our wisdom.

Self-knowledge can make us aware of the personal and public journey that women have lived. The attainment of equal rights shows itself in educational opportunities, the right to vote, and the right to work. But none of that history comes alive until we acknowledge, learn, and understand our own personal story, and the story of our ancestors. For most of our ancestors and our family, *feminist* was not a word known or used. That doesn't diminish the fact that women in our families paved a way and paid a price for our benefit. Their history is the deep hum of encouragement and support that vibrates through our current lives.

I think of my mother, my grandmother, and my great-grandmother as the angels in my life who have helped me. The story my mother chose to tell me under the featherbed quilt in Grandmother Julia's guest room about dolls in the attic was about women living on their own, without outside interference from the world of men. It was just a fantasy then, but now women can and do claim their own power, especially in midlife, and that's the real story.

The women in our families who came before us do this: they shine the light of inspiration on us. And the journey that we undertake is not only for ourselves. We do it for ourselves and for the sake of our daughters, our granddaughters, and our nieces.

There are other stories, too, ones we'd do well not to forget. They are the stories of struggle, of wanting to be seen, heard, and treated as capable and equal. I have worked hard at being respected and taken seriously. My strength, ambition, and courage were what I thought to be admirable qualities. Through the process of maturing, my heart revealed that I desired to live life on my own terms. So I began to demand authenticity from myself. I worked on approval as coming from within me and not from an outside source. It's not been a smooth journey. Like all big changes we grow into, I lumbered and lurched toward my ideal in a clunky manner. I've betrayed myself many times in order to keep the peace or the status quo, or simply because I didn't know how to handle certain situations.

I can recall times when some men, that unevolved Neanderthal type of man, would insult me with a barrage of sexual innuendo or even blatant objectification. I had trouble finding the right words to put those people in their place, and I often didn't know what action to take. Like many women of my generation, the stories I shared of these encounters were whispered in quiet, embarrassed tones in the ladies' room, only to be chalked up as "boys will be boys" and followed with "just let it go."

I learned what it was to be passed over for a job because I was "a girl." I am familiar with being left out of the conversation because of my gender. I've been called a "fucking bitch" and worse. And I've witnessed public figures with wide bandwidth and amplified airtime admonish and label women who weren't compliant, childlike Barbies as *feminazis*. The scenarios I describe are not mine alone. They belong to the story of women, one marked by a terrible, horrible, and yet beautiful grappling of finding our voice and our power.

Our struggles have not been in vain, however, though many times I felt that cultural changes and shifts were taking longer than they should. When I compare my generation to my mother's and my grandmother's, I can see how far we've come. It's not just the historical progression that I look at, but the arc of my own life and how I grew into a confident woman with a sense of purpose.

The old archetypal arc was one of Maiden/Mother/Crone, or we could say innocence/Madonna/hag. The emerging archetype of Creatrix redefines that progression and most especially redefines and relegates the Crone to her place in the shadows.

When I think of the old progression, I can't imagine any young woman today referring to herself as a maiden. The word *maiden* is associated with being nonmarried, with purity, virginity, and chastity. All those words suggest male ownership over a woman's body. It's a battle we still fight. *Maiden* is the kind of label one might expect to find in a fairy tale in which women are princesses who need rescuing. But in real life, young women are capable and aware. The twentysomethings I've met have a much greater sense of power and leadership than my generation did.

Similarly with motherhood. Some of the older definitions of motherhood relate more to saintly Madonnas, desexualized and placed upon a pedestal of purity and parenting for men to idolize. But that's not what motherhood is these days. The mothers I know encourage their daughters and sons to recognize equality and greatness. They model independence and resiliency. In most cases, women who are mothers also have a career outside the home. All of it comes down to this: mothers are more than mothers.

The archetype of Creatrix is one that is not defined by a man, but by women. *Creatrix* means "a woman who makes things." For me, the name conjures images of claiming the mature, self-confident, and wise midlife woman, breathing into her new life and greater creativity. While I've written this book to shine a light on the qualities of this emerging archetype, I'm hoping there are women out there who will do the same with the old ideas of maiden and motherhood. We no longer live in a world where we can let others define us.

We spend our entire lives in a state of becoming human beings, an endeavor none of us ever truly master. Recognition of this new archetype is one thing, but integrating the Creatrix is quite another. How do we begin?

We need to rethink what's too often referred to as a midlife crisis for women, a time of weakness and hysteria, to become instead a period of midlife awakening. Women have been imagining and reimagining their lives for centuries as we marched toward liberation. Reinvention and reimagination is never a crisis. It is a step toward becoming aware of our greatest potential and taking action upon that. When we reinvent ourselves, we are being proactive in our own evolution. Therefore, awakening is never a destination point but is part of the ongoing process of becoming human. May we continue to grow psychologically and spiritually until the day we die!

Acknowledging the Creatrix in our lives is an invitation to celebrate our stories and our lives. There is a great power in women coming together to tell their stories, not in the lamentation of lost youth, but in the ceremony of celebration for the accumulating years and wisdom that result. Sharing our voices in story is one of the ways we begin to integrate the Creatrix and embody her. Writing down or telling our story allows us to better own our power and strength. Women who share their personal stories, who bear witness to stories of other women, give the gift of encouragement.

The images from our girlhoods hold countless clues as to how we view being a midlife woman. My grandmother Julia and my mother, Cleo, both had a sense of independence, but they also had a sense of when to be compliant or obedient to certain men in their lives. Julia knew how to kill a chicken and cook it for dinner. She could lift heavy bags of grain out of a truck when she was eighty. She was strong, both physically and mentally. Julia was a spiritual mentor to me. I admired her strength and wanted to be like her, but she was also married to a man who drank too much and hit her at times. Even with all her strength and independence, she would have never dreamed of giving her husband an ultimatum or leaving him. She was of a time when women had few places to go if they left their husbands, and anyplace they might find refuge, they'd most likely be marked as a fallen woman.

Cleo did leave her husband and was harshly judged for that action. Though she grew into her independence and authority with a kind of courage and determination not usually seen in women of her generation, she longed for another marriage, because marriage was what made her feel like she belonged. Once she remarried, she left behind the career woman she'd been and became a compliant wife, content to refer to herself as "just a housewife." I tried to challenge this, saying to her often, "Mom, you're not married to a house." She'd smile and reply, "Your generation is different, sweetie." She was right: my generation was different. Still, I saw how my mom paved the way for me to be more than what she or my grandmother Julia had been allowed to even dream.

It's an honor to have witnessed the past fifty years of feminist history. We've come so far—and have so much farther to go. A new light shines within us, evidenced by the accomplishments and kindness of midlife women all around us.

The stories of our grandmothers and our mothers are where we begin to integrate the emerging archetype of the Creatrix. The stories of women who live their lives on larger stages hold significance for us, too. You don't have to look too far to see the embodiment of the Creatrix story in the likes of Carole King, Ruth Bader Ginsburg, Meryl Streep, or Reese Witherspoon. Those larger-than-life women are certainly a great source of inspiration, but we must reach into ourselves to find our personal story. We need to share those stories for the sake of legacy, as well as our self-knowledge.

When I was a girl, my mother made up stories that she told me at bedtime, so my first reference to stories was as a world outside of myself. Then, in my midthirties, I began to realize there was a story inside of me, too, one in which I was the heroine of the journey. That is the story that every woman has inside of herself.

Every single day, we need to remind ourselves that we matter. As clichéd as it may sound, we need to love ourselves, and we do this through learning the stories that make up our life and connect us to the lives of our ancestors. This sense of soulfulness that comes from being the storyteller—it's our gift. It's what we give to the next generation.

Let's not forget our history and the amazing distance we've traveled. Let's not forget that women's history resides within us and within our very own families. May we continue to celebrate women in this generosity of spirit and potential.

There is an overarching message for us all as we become midlife women: You've been passed a torch. Now you hold that light to help not only yourself, but other women as well. It's time to name and claim your power. Don't let anyone define your capabilities, your intelligence, your thoughtfulness, or your creativity by your years. Do your soul work. Embrace the beauty and grace of age and its gifts of wisdom. Make life on your own terms. You are never too old to dream, to participate, to engage. Uplift other women. Tell your story. You are at the front of the line now. Hold your light high, and be proud of who you are and who you are still becoming. Accept the mantle of Creatrix, and celebrate the goodness and the grace that it holds.

For Reflection, Activity, and Journaling

Telling your story creates a platform for your deepest longings, fears, and loves to be revealed. Story helps you see what it is you believe, what you're willing to fight for, and most importantly, what is truly in your heart. You've reflected, contemplated, and been presented with questions throughout this book. Those can help you now as you gather together the pieces of your own precious story.

Story is an homage to the life we create. *Who am I* is a question that asks more than *Who do I want to be?* or *What do I want to have?* It asks us to dig into our heart and psyche and uncover the secrets that go beyond wanting to be kind, wild, and creative.

We all have secrets that we dare not speak for fear of having to own them once and for all. These secrets are not about the time that you took five dollars out of Aunt Mary's purse when you were fourteen. They're not about the boy you kissed when you knew your best girlfriend liked him so much. No, these are the secrets that whisper how good and deserving we are, how creative and kind our spirit is. I cannot let myself die without releasing the burden of keeping those things secret from myself, so I make them a story. I cannot die without mining those whispers that jar me awake in the middle of the night with a dream of light streaming through a window. I have to own them through the power of personal story, and in that way, story becomes an act of self-love.

Our lives are made up of stories, quests that change, challenge, and empower us, reminders that this is the *sacred* journey that we call life. You can tell your story to yourself just for its own sake. Or you can share your story in a circle of friends, where they have the opportunity to share their story, too. You can write down your story. You can make a small legacy book for your family or friends. Art or photographs can be included. Or you can record the telling of your story or write a song about a slice of your life. You might become a podcaster, which is a new way of telling story. Telling your story will teach you things about yourself, and when you can see yourself as the heroine of your own journey, that story becomes a liberating force.

The Heroine's Journey: A Possible Outline

Where to begin? Below I've given you an idea for how to construct your story. These are based on the Hero's Journey as first laid out by author and mythologist Joseph Campbell and then made applicable for writers by Christopher Vogler in his book *The Writer's Journey.*

Start with this writing prompt: Once upon a time, you were going about life, minding your own business, and then—

1. Because of some event (which is what your story is about), you are set upon a quest. It's a call to adventure that will remove you, the heroine, from your familiar environment.

2. Initially, you (remember, you're the heroine) try to escape the call to adventure. You have a difficult choice to make, but maybe the choice is worth it.

3. You meet a helper or two along the way.

4. You leave the ordinary world and find yourself in an extraordinary world.

5. You are tested as you meet allies and enemies.

6. You reach a turning point and are awakened, ready to be the warrior and fight the necessary battle.

7. You face your greatest fear.

8. You, as the heroine, are transformed and driven to complete the journey.

9. You bring home the prize. The prize can be a lesson learned, or it can be something tangible. I had a friend who wrote about a pear-shaped ring that was passed from generation to generation in her family. In the end, the ring was willed to her, and she understood its full significance.

Though this is a classic structure for memoir and storytelling, you can shuffle these ideas around as you tell your tale. Don't worry if your story doesn't include all of these elements. Often women narrate their thoughts not realizing that the classic components of the heroine's journey are naturally there. The most important thing is that you speak honestly and not shy away from any of the emotions that are part of the telling.

Resources for Telling Your Story

Here are some resources that might be useful: *Writing Down the Bones* and *Old Friend from Far Away*, both by Natalie Goldberg. I'm a longtime Natalie Goldberg fan. She's written several books that get the writing juices flowing, but even if you don't write your story, the Goldberg prompts can help you tell your story through recording, sharing, or photographs.

One of my favorite writers is May Sarton. I still have a battered copy of *Journal of a Solitude* that sits on the table next to my writing chair. What I find so helpful about May Sarton is how she writes the truth about her day-to-day life. She feels so honest and so accessible, like someone you could sit down with for an in-depth conversation.

And finally, a website: www.storycircle.org. This is for a national organization called Story Circle Network, which encourages women to share their stories.

◆ ◆ ◆

Each woman has a unique history that's made up of many small stories. Sharing your chronicles with others is a way of sharing your heart and your soul. It's also the way in which you've been growing into the archetype of the Creatrix. Your narratives are what connect you to other women and to your shared humanity. Every woman I've ever known has a tale to tell that is brave and beautiful, sad and sweet. Knowing your stories and those of women around you can change the way you see the world, and even change the world, as you become the Creatrix.

THE GIFT OF COVID-19: FROM THE PERSPECTIVE OF THE CREATRIX

The voice and energy of the Creatrix rising is not an isolated phenomenon. So much of the cultural shift, anxiety, and unrest in these times is due to the presence of the Coronavirus (Covid-19) pandemic. We are all living through a great uprising that has stirred up messages that have lingered on the edges of our society and have now been given a light in which to stand, be seen, and be heard. This includes women reimagining their leadership roles while rejecting the toxic myths of aging, as well as our Black brothers and sisters demanding social justice and equality while simultaneously demonstrating courage and conviction. The white world has finally shut up and is starting to listen. None of us can deny any longer the sheer force of numbers with regard to people who seek a deeper and more meaningful connection with the world and with each other.

What is also evident during this time is that the voices rising within us and around us could not have happened to such a large degree without the presence of this currently raging pandemic. When viewed from the perspective of a story, with the Coronavirus personified and playing the main character, the event becomes a tale of sorrow, caution, and inspiration. To this end, story gives us the ability to gather into our psyche more than just the data of this world event. We are able to examine the symbols of the event and take to heart a story of how we might become better, wiser, and more compassionate and connected people—because story mimics life.

In this story, the Creatrix is emerging along with other cultural changes, and it is a hard journey. But the potential of such a tale is that the heroine of the story will experience transformation.

The Story of Corona

Corona was not invited to the party in New York City that night in late December of 2019, but she showed up anyway. Tight red dress, hair immaculately done, skin luminous and smooth, she turned heads when she walked into the room, and everyone gasped, unable to take their eyes off her. It took a great deal of time for someone to remark, "Who is that? Is she on the guest list?" That question left many of the party guests scrambling for answers. Was she a friend of the mayor? Of the governor? What brought her to New York? And why didn't anyone here know who she was? The woman with the commanding presence would soon be known to all of them.

That's how it began. One party. One late night. Guests dressed up and sipping champagne. Not a care in the world. Those same guests, upon arriving home, could not stop talking about her. They went to bed but could not sleep. Instead they tossed and turned, unable to shake the idea that they had some connection to the woman in the red dress, that they'd seen her before.

Days later, the same people grew tired and weak. They stayed home. A cough. Just a cold. Now they slept but only with dreams of the woman in the red dress, who, in each of their dreams, was kneeling upon their chest, her long fingernails pressing into their skin. Had anyone noticed her hands before? Her nails? The brightly shellacked manicure with fingernails shaped like hooks that stung ever so slightly when she'd reached out to shake their hand. She'd said her name was Corona, a Spanish name meaning *crown*, she'd told them. It was a name that would stay with them, that would be on their lips when they died.

Early on, before her name became famous, she loitered in small dark places and alleyways. The places where people rise early to work, running to catch subways and buses, returning late at night, exhausted from what the day took from them. She followed their steps, got on the same bus, rode the same crowded service elevators. And always, she was dressed to impress, every hair in place and that gorgeous skin of hers. No one could ever look away, and so many people were eager to shake hands with her. As they did, each would feel the slight pinch of her hooklike nails puncturing their flesh.

Corona became world-famous in a short amount of time. On each hand she had so graciously taken into her own upon meeting, there grew new hook-shaped nails, just like hers. Each of those souls went forth and shook the hand of another. The more she put herself at the center of attention, the more her breath became sweet and heavy. She would lean over those to whom she'd been recently introduced, and the seductive warm smell of her breath made them lean forward as if to inhale her.

Corona noted there were certain people, higher-up people, who disregarded her and disrespected her. They gave speeches about her: "Just ignore this woman. She'll go away. You'll see. It will be a beautiful miracle. She will just go away." Hearing this angered Corona greatly. She would not be dismissed so easily. She demanded respect.

The respect came in the form of admonishments to keep your distance. Wash your hands, and the hooklike nails would fade away. "Don't let her be the death of you," said a man in a white coat. He understood this was how to respect her, and in turn, Corona respected him. And still, there were those who would not acknowledge her power or listen to the warnings.

More and more people became sick, unable to understand that Corona had come to us with a consciousness and an intent. Some people began to study her. They wanted to understand, so they kept their distance and managed to prevent her hooklike nails from getting into them. They tended the sick and warned that Corona would infect us all if we didn't respect her. She wanted to make us die, they said. Even though a trail of death and sickness followed wherever she went, her intent was far broader than the singular desire for our death.

In the beginning, none of us could have imagined her larger intent. And the leader who promised that Corona was just going to go away laid down an edict to all people in the land: "Stay home. Stay away from other people. Lock your doors so Corona does not find you." And we did. And for a time, it seemed like she might fade into the distance.

Corona then surprised us. She knew she would find a way to draw us out of our homes. What no one knew was that Corona could make light. It was not the kind of light enjoyed in bathing under a sun. It was not the soft, blue light of the moon. It was not the light that's meant when someone signs a note, "love and light." It was an interrogator's light. We hadn't realized that while more people were getting sick, the light Corona shined onto us was getting brighter.

When the warmth and the promise of summer came, no one wanted to stay inside any longer. In the grand scheme of things, had that many people died? If no one died that we knew, maybe it was just an overblown hoax. And this attitude caused Corona to shine her light of interrogation even brighter.

People began to see what her light was shining upon: everything that was broken in our world. Every fissure and crack of cruelty, racism, poverty, and greed came into full view and stunned our senses and sensibilities.

One day, Corona sat on a curb and watched as a Black man was murdered in the street by another man kneeling on his neck. A child filmed it on her phone for everyone to see. A wound broke open, and its oozing content flooded the airwaves. This is how Black men die. When this man died, he called out for his mother. And what was heard around the world was a call to all mothers.

Corona knew this would bring people out of their homes. In addition to her interrogator's light shining on all the broken places, it also shined on a soft spot in the human heart, a place of hope, a place of better angels where people want to connect and come together in the name of love.

So out the front door streamed individuals of every color and age, taking to the streets. They cried out, "Black lives matter!" Someone tried to say, "No, all lives matter." But the mother energy invoked by the murdered Black man whipped around to the sound of where that statement came from and pointed a finger.

"All lives cannot matter until Black lives matter," the mother energy said.

People marched. Women. Men. Children. White. Black. All shades of colors together. All ages. They marched in masks to keep the Corona breath away.

Those that studied Corona worked at a breakneck speed. They would find a way to inoculate the population against her. Just a vaccine. A treatment. A cure. It has to happen. The mother energy of the world knew, however, that the cure for our suffering wasn't to be found entirely in vaccines or treatments. While those things can send the woman in the red dress packing, we'd be fools to not heed the lesson she came here to impart.

The voice of midlife women, the voice of this emerging archetype of Creatrix, has been heightened by Corona. Corona has helped us witness the voice of Black Americans so they can finally be heard. And we, as a culture that has been asleep, blind, and turned away from so many of society's ills, are starting to get out of the way of our own assumptions, and just shut up. The voice of poverty has given us a reason to pause and ask how we can have a world that works for everyone.

Was it Corona's intent to awaken us to our better angels? To show us that we cannot continue to live in a place where only some people matter? Was her message to tell women to stand strong and make their voices heard, to address issues of poverty and prejudice? Corona was not invited to the party, but the door was left wide open for her to enter. She changed the world with her harsh interrogating light and her indifference to past beliefs. She showed us what was broken and challenged us to heal the deep wounds of bigotry, greed, inequality, and despair.

Corona invited the mothers, the woman warriors, and every Creatrix rising to step forward and make a difference, to embrace our power, our wisdom, and our love. She invited us to stand in the light of leadership and make this world what we know it can be.

Now is the time to accept that invitation.

—November 2020

Acknowledgments

I am grateful for the gift of storytelling and the gift of writing. As such, I'm also grateful to those people in my life who have taught, supported, counseled, loved, encouraged, and cheered me on in my endeavor to tell stories.

Always first on my list is my husband, Dean, who is my biggest cheerleader and very best friend. Thank you, sweetest heart, for reading and rereading my stuff, for the discussions, ideas, and humor. Walking this life with you is my great joy and privilege.

Thank you to my kindred spirit of an editor and friend, Nancy Marriott. You've made me a better writer, a better student, and a better human being. Thanks to Susannah Noel for your sense of detail and nuance, and for making me look good. Working with you has been both eye-opening and heart opening.

Profound appreciation and goodwill to all the women at She Writes Press. My deep admiration for the indomitable business acumen of Brooke Warner, who keeps forging the path to help women tell their stories. And thank you to my project manager, Shannon Green, for her positive attitude and sense of play. Round two with you was even more fun than the first.

Thank you to the women at Books Forward for hanging in there with me: Marissa DeCuir, Julie Schoerke, Angelle Barbazon, and the digital lady dynamo, Brittany Kennell!

To my writing buddies, who keep me sane, inspire my heart, and always have time for a cuppa, I owe you deep appreciation: G. Z. Hill, Jennifer Egan, and Jeanne Guy. Your work inspires my own and I feel so blessed to have you in my life!

Thank you to Joe McNair, Ph.D., for the counsel, guidance and insight, and a picture window into myth and how our stories connect us. You have enriched my life in so many ways.

Very special thanks to Reverend Cynthia James for her patient instruction. You believed in me before I believed in myself. And to the great poet, Richard Blanco, who was crucial to a great transformative part of my story, thank you.

Thank you to my great niece, Nancy Ann Picucci, for always reassuring me that I have a family to which I belong.

Last, and certainly not least, thank you to the two women who steadfastly remain close at heart and never fail to make me laugh and remind me to have a good time. You are dear jockettes in my life and because of you, I've spent more time on the trail than I ever dreamed I would. Thank you Taffy Pelton and Elisa Kohls-Pedersen.

ABOUT THE AUTHOR

S tephanie Raffelock is the author of *A Delightful Little Book on Aging* (She Writes Press, 2020). A graduate of Naropa University's program in writing and poetics, she has worked as a freelancer for *The Aspen Times* and *The Rogue Valley Messenger* and has written and blogged for *Nexus Magazine, Omaha Lifestyles,* Care2.com, and SixtyandMe. com, to name a few. She is a popular public speaker for employment relations groups and has given national keynotes for Breaking the Glass as well as Charles Schwab on the topic of feminist history. A recent transplant to Austin, Texas, Stephanie enjoys an active life with her husband, Dean, and their Labrador retriever, Mickey.

Author photo © Tara Pottichen

SELECTED TITLES FROM SHE WRITES PRESS

She Writes Press is an independent publishing company founded to serve women writers everywhere. Visit us at www.shewritespress.com.

A Delightful Little Book on Aging by Stephanie Raffelock. $19.95, 978-1-63152-840-8. A collection of thoughts and stories woven together with a fresh philosophy that helps to dispel some of the toxic stereotypes of aging, this inspirational, empowering, and emotionally honest look at life's journey is part joyful celebration and part invitation to readers to live life fully to the very end.

Winter's Graces: The Surprising Gifts of Later Life by Susan Avery Stewart, PhD. $16.95, 978-1-63152-379-3. A heartening and engaging guide to the surprising gifts of later life, based on ancient stories, recent research, elders' lived experience, the world's spiritual traditions, and the author's thirty-plus years as a psychology professor and psychotherapist.

The Book of Old Ladies: Celebrating Women of a Certain Age in Fiction by Ruth O. Saxton. $16.95, 978-1-63152-797-5. In this book lover's guide to approaching old age and its losses while still embracing beauty, sensuality, creativity, connection, wonder, and joy, Ruth Saxton introduces readers to thirty modern stories featuring "women of a certain age" who prepare for the journey of aging, inhabit the territory, and increasingly become their truest selves.

Love, Life, and Lucille: Lessons Learned from a Centenarian by Judy Gaman. $16.95, 978-1-63152-882-8. Judy, a feisty, fortysomething professional trapped in the unrelenting world of workaholism, forges an incredible bond with a centenarian—and life takes on a whole new meaning for both of them.

The Shelf Life of Ashes: A Memoir by Hollis Giammatteo. $16.95, 978-1-63152-047-1. Confronted by an importuning mother 3,000 miles away who thinks her end is nigh—and feeling ambushed by her impending middle age—Giammatteo determines to find The Map of Aging Well, a decision that leads her on an often-comic journey.

CPSIA information can be obtained
at www.ICGtesting.com
Printed in the USA
LVHW041212120621
689955LV00001B/1/J

9 781647 423186